Kierkegaardian
Philosophy in
THE FAITH
of a
SCHOLAR

KIERKEGAARDIAN

PHILOSOPHY IN

THE FAITH

of a

SCHOLAR

David F. Swenson
Edited by Lillian M. Swenson

THE WESTMINSTER PRESS
Philadelphia

PRINTED IN THE UNITED STATES OF AMERICA

To Those Former Students
of
DAVID F. SWENSON
Who Still Cherish His Teachings

Preface

IN HIS later years David F. Swenson derived a quiet satisfaction from the knowledge that while he was still a young and inexperienced teacher he had been able to recognize in Søren Kierkegaard one of the great thinkers of the world. Shortly after beginning his work as an assistant in the department of philosophy at the University of Minnesota, in 1898, he discovered in a local library a philosophical book in Danish by an author whose name was wholly unknown to him. Because it was philosophy, he took the book, which chanced to be Kierkegaard's *Unscientific Postscript,* home with him, and read it completely through during the next twenty-four hours. As he read, David F. Swenson became one of the first English thinkers to recognize the genius of a writer whose works now, fifty years later, are coming to have an ever increasing interest in philosophical and theological thinking.

From that time on, Mr. Swenson read and reread whatever of Kierkegaard he could lay hold of. Himself the possessor of a naturally logical and dialectical mind, he found Kierkegaard's writings to be not only logical and dialectical to a supreme degree, but expressed with a wit, pathos, irony, humor, and passion unusual in a philosophical work. During the ensuing years he continued to absorb himself in and assimilate Kierkegaard's thought and, as far as might be, to acquaint others with it in conversations and classroom lectures.

In 1914, in a course sponsored by the University of Minnesota on " Great Thinkers of the Nineteenth Century," he
gave his first public address on Kierkegaard. This was, I believe, the first public address on Kierkegaard in English ever
delivered in this country. Mr. Swenson characterized the fundamental note of the Danish thinker's message to the world
as the idea that the truth is not objective but subjective. He
pointed out that Kierkegaard himself had recognized that
his task was to " clothe the Christian religion in the garb of
philosophical reflection, without modification or distortion,
complete and entire," and that he had predicted that his ultimate significance would depend "absolutely on the fate of
Christianity."

For the next twenty years Mr. Swenson was carrying on
his one-man effort to make the English world acquainted
with the name and thought of Kierkegaard. A partial list of
his activities in this direction shows him speaking before the
most varied groups — ministerial associations, women's clubs,
college and high school commencement classes, theological
seminaries, rationalist and historical societies, and philosophical association meetings — and preaching in churches of various denominations. But whatever his topic, like Socrates in
the *Gorgias,* he always managed to say the same things
about the same, and to import into his talks a stiff dose of
Kierkegaard's ethical and religious philosophy. A single lecture might include ideas gleaned from half a dozen or more
of Kierkegaard's works, not as quotations, but as themes as-
similated into his own thinking. Essentially he was a speaker
rather than a writer; and he was at his best in this role since
he was eloquent with the passion of his conviction, not
through rhetorical flourishes. A half page of notepaper con-
taining a few scribbled notes sufficed for an evening's lecture.
Only his more formal presentations were written out, and he

himself felt that they lost much of their spontaneity when he was forced to read them.

Thus he was for many years a solitary voice. But he was from the first concerned with the urgent need of having this new philosophy made available for English readers. The project involved many difficulties. Not only were the writings locked up in the Danish language, but the subject matter was difficult, and Kierkegaard's poetic genius clothed it in a literary style impossible for a lesser writer to translate adequately. With these difficulties in mind, Mr. Swenson began his twofold task: first, to make sure that he really understood Kierkegaard's thought; and next, to train himself in a literary form of expression which, while it could not reproduce Kierkegaard's genius, might yet convey to the reader some conception of the vivid imagery, the poetic imagination, and the vigorous polemic of this greatest of Denmark's prose writers. Incidentally, he was also developing his own literary style, with the somewhat ironical result that when he finally came to publish, it was at times difficult for a reader to know how much was Kierkegaard and how much was Swenson. He would have been the last to claim that his style was that of Kierkegaard, but it did represent his best efforts to create a dignity and vividness of expression not inconsonant with that of Kierkegaard. So it is that his papers on subjects unrelated to Kierkegaard reflect what many, familiar with his writing, have come to characterize as the "Kierkegaard style." It has been said that Mr. Swenson's writings have at times a certain "elusive" quality, which Kierkegaard would have called a "deceptive character," inasmuch as some things appear very simple to one reading them casually, until one suddenly awakens to the realization that something very profound has been said. This influence of Kierkegaard on Mr. Swenson's style is worth emphasizing, lest some who did not know him might feel that he was appropriating Kierkegaard's thoughts as his own.

The lectures reproduced in this volume do not deal directly with Kierkegaard, but they may be understood best in the light of the profound influence of Kierkegaard on his thinking and expression. For example, the theme of one of the most weighty addresses in this collection, " Objective Uncertainty and Human Faith," is derived from Kierkegaard's *Unscientific Postscript.* The purpose of the address on supernaturalism, moreover, was to delineate one of the sources of Kierkegaard's moral power. Quotations from Kierkegaard and some of the more obvious allusions to his thoughts have been identified in notes at the end of this book.

The addresses included in the following pages were given at various times and upon various occasions during a ten-year period between 1927 and 1936. In spite of the variety of circumstances and the time span involved, however, these lectures have in them a marked unity both in respect to a consistent philosophic point of view and a deep and unwavering Christian faith. Those who have heard these addresses, or have read them in the periodicals in which some of them appeared originally, have seen in them both a historic and a contemporary significance. For the sake of the history of American thought, it is not unimportant to make permanent record of the fact that in the 1920's and 1930's when so much of the prevailing philosophy found little or no place for faith in God and when a considerable portion of theology was noticeably humanistic in tone, there was at least one thinker voicing a new, and at that time little-appreciated, philosophy that was distinctly Christian.

LILLIAN M. SWENSON

Contents

I   The Dignity of Human Life   13

II   Progress in Religious Thought   29

III   Evolution and Life Values   49

IV   Functions of Intelligence   83

V   Objective Uncertainty and Human Faith   96

VI   Supernaturalism — Source of Moral Power   131

VII   The Transforming Power of Otherworldliness   145

NOTES   160

I

The Dignity of Human Life

This address was delivered originally on June 3, 1929, at Gustavus Adolphus College and was used at other places later. It has never before been published.

MAN LIVES forward, but he thinks backward. As an active being, his task is to press forward to the things that are before, toward the goal where is the prize of the high calling. But as a thinking, active being, his forward movement is conditioned by a retrospect. If there were no past for a man, there could be no future; and if there were no future and no past, but only such an immersion in the present as is characteristic of the brute which perisheth, then there would be nothing eternal in human life, and everything distinctively and essentially human would disappear from our existence.

As a preparation for an existence in the present, the youth of a nation are trained in various skills and along devious lines, according to their capacities and circumstances, for the parts they are to play in existence; their natural talents are developed, some by extended periods of intellectual training, others for participation in various forms of business or technical training; but whatever be the ultimate end of the training, its purpose is to develop those latent powers they possess which will eventually prove of benefit to themselves or to others. But, in addition to this, which we may call a preparation for the external life, a something else is urgently needed, a something so fundamentally important that in its absence every other form of preparation is revealed as imperfect and incomplete, even ineffective and futile.

This so particularly indispensable something is a view of life, and a view of life is not acquired as a direct and immediate result of a course of study, the reading of books, or a communication of results. It is wholly a product of the individual's own knowledge of himself as an individual, of his individual capabilities and aspirations. A view of life is a principle of living, a spirit and an attitude capable of maintaining its unity and identity with itself in all of life's complexities and varying vicissitudes; and yet also capable of being declined, to use the terminology of the grammatical sciences, in all the infinite variety of cases that the language of life affords. Without this preparation the individual life is like a ship without a rudder, a bit of wreckage floating with the current to an uncomprehended destiny. A view of life is not objective knowledge, but subjective conviction. It is a part of a man's own self, the source whence the stream of his life issues. It is the dominant attitude of the spirit which gives to life its direction and its goal. This is why it cannot be directly communicated or conveyed, like an article of commerce, from one person to another. If a view of life were a body of knowledge about life, or a direct and immediate implication from such knowledge, it would be subject to objective communication and systematic instruction. But it is rather a personal expression of what a man essentially is in his own inmost self, and this cannot be learned by rote, or accepted at the hands of some external authority. Knowledge is the answer or answers that things give to the questions we ask of them; a view of life is the reply a person gives to the question that life asks of him. We

begin life by scrutinizing our environment, ourselves play-
ing the role of questioners and examiners and critics; but
at a later moment, when the soul comes of age and is about
to enter upon its majority, it learns that the tables have
been turned and the roles reversed; from that moment it
confronts a question, a searching and imperative question,
in relation to which no evasion can avail, and to which no
shifting of responsibility is possible.

In discussing the problem of a view of life which can give
it meaning and dignity and worth, I am well aware that
no one can acquire a view of life by listening to a speech.
Nevertheless, a speech may serve the more modest purpose
of stimulating a search, perhaps a more earnest search; and
may render more articulate possibly the convictions of those
who have already won some such conception, having made
it their own by a heartfelt and spontaneous choice.

All men are endowed by nature with a desire for happiness — a principle so obvious as scarcely to need any explanation, and certainly no defense. A human life without
happiness or hope of happiness is not a life, but rather a
death in life. Happiness is life's vital fluid and the very
breath of its nostrils. Happiness and life are so much one
and the same thing that the more profoundly any life discovers happiness, the more significant and abundant is that
life itself. This is also the principle of the Christian religion, which even dares to formulate the task of life as the
duty of being happy; for does not the Apostle Paul say,
"Rejoice . . . always: again I will say, Rejoice"? So deeply
grounded in human nature is the need for happiness, that
the desire for it is not only universal and instinctive, but in-
eradicable and imperative. Man is made for happiness; an
essentially unhappy man has missed his goal, and has failed
to realize his humanity.

But for a thinking human being — and God made every man a thinker, whatever may be our estimate of that which men make of themselves — for a thinking human being, happiness cannot consist in the satisfaction of momentary impulse, of blind feeling, of brute immediacy. A pleasant absorption in the present, oblivious of prospect or retrospect, careless of the wider relations or the deeper truth of life, can be called happiness only on the basis of frivolity and thoughtlessness. Just as life is not life unless it is happy, so happiness is not happiness unless it can be justified. In order really to be happiness it requires to be interpenetrated with a sense of meaning, reason, and worth.

For the quest for happiness, like every other human quest, faces a danger. The danger that confronts it is the possibility of error: the error of permitting oneself to be lured into promising paths that lead to no goal, and the error of coming to rest in hollow satisfactions and empty joys. It is possible to believe oneself happy, to seem happy to oneself and to others, and yet in reality to be plunged in the deepest misery; just as, on the other hand, it is possible to stand possessed of the greatest treasure, and yet, in thoughtlessness, to imagine oneself destitute, and through that very thoughtlessness not only neglect and ignore but actually deprive oneself of what one already has. The basic problem of life, the question in response to which a view of life seeks to propound an answer, may therefore be formulated as follows: What is that happiness which is also a genuine and lasting good? In what does it consist, and how may it be attained?

There exists an ancient handbook, an *Art of Rhetoric,* compiled for the guidance and information of orators and other public speakers, written by one of the greatest of Greek philosophers. In this handbook the author formulates the commonly prevailing conceptions of happiness as among the things useful for public speakers to know. This textbook is almost twenty-five hundred years old, and the views it presents on this subject may therefore be expected to seem childish in the light of our greater insight and extraordinary progress in all things. Nevertheless, let us note them in passing, if only for the sake of seeing how far we have advanced beyond them. Happiness is said to be commonly defined as independence of life, as prosperity with virtue, as comfortable circumstances with security, or as the enjoyment of many possessions, together with the power to keep and defend them. Its constituent elements are noble birth, wealth, many good and influential friends, bodily health and beauty, talents and capacities, good fortune, honors, and lastly virtue. We readily perceive how strange and old-fashioned these conceptions are, how foreign to all our modern and enlightened notions. I shall therefore subjoin a more up-to-date consideration of the same subject, derived from a very modern author writing in a journal of today. The author raises the question as to what circumstances and conditions have the power to make him feel really alive, tingling with vitality, instinct with the joy of living. He submits a long list including a variety of things, of which I shall quote the chief: the sense of health; successful creative work, like writing books; good food and drink; pleasant surroundings; praise, not spread on too thick; friends and their company; beautiful things, books, music; athletic exercises and sports; daydreaming; a good fight in a tolerably decent cause; the sense of bodily danger escaped; the consciousness of being a few steps ahead of the wolf of poverty. His social ideal is a community where beauty abounds, where the fear of want is absent, where a man may dress as he pleases, do the work that suits him best; a community where arts and letters flourish, where abundant leisure breaks the remorseless pace of ceaseless work, and, lastly, for those who value religion, a church is provided, with a great nave and a great organ and the sound of vespers across the evening fields. So speaks our modern writer. And now that I have juxtaposed these two accounts, I have to confess to the strange feeling that, despite the interval of more than two thousand years between them, they sound unexpectedly alike, even to the generous inclusion of a place for morality and religion as not an entirely negligible factor in promoting the good and happy life. How strange to find such a similarity! Can it be that after all that has been said and written about the revolutionary and radical changes introduced into life by modern science, modern invention, and modern industry, the influence of the steam engine and the printing press, the telegraph and the radio, the automobile and the airplane, together with the absolutely devastating discoveries of astronomers — can it be, in spite of all this, that the current conceptions of life and its meaning have remained essentially unchanged? Is not this a remarkable testimony to the profound inner resemblance to one another, despite all changes of form and circumstance, exhibited by the countless generations of men, both in their wisdom and in their folly?

However that may be, I do not think that anyone will deny that such views as these are widely held, and constitute the view of life perhaps of the majority of men. The testimony to their prevalence is not merely the articulate confession of the tongue, but the no less revealing though inarticulate direction of the life. I hope not to be misunderstood. The present speaker is human enough to find these objectives, or the majority of them, not only natural but inviting; he finds them desirable, and is by no means schooled in any heroic or stoic indifference to the goods that have rightly been called external, rooted as they are in fortunate circumstances and special privilege. But there are serious difficulties in the way of constructing a view of life out of such considerations.

The constituents of happiness are in both cases a multiplicity of things. As Aristotle so simply says, virtue alone will not make a man happy, but he needs also goods and friends. But the self which sets its heart upon any such multiplicity of external goods, which lives in them and by them and for them, dependent upon them for the only happiness it knows — such a self is captive to the diverse world of its desires. It belongs to the world and does not own itself. It is not in the deepest sense a self, since it is not free and is not a unity. The manifold conditions of its happiness split the self asunder; no ruling passion dominates its life; no concentration gives unity to the personality and single-mindedness to the will. Its name is legion, and its nature is double-mindedness. And if some one thing, like wealth or power, is made the single ambition of an exceptional life, it still remains true that such things are only apparently single; in reality they are various and manifold. The soul that lives in them is torn by diverse impulses, is drawn in many different directions at once, and cannot find the peace which comes only from single-minded devotion, from the pursuit of an end which is intrinsically and genuinely one.

Reflection discovers yet another difficulty in connection with such views of life. Whoever seeks his happiness in external conditions, of whatever sort, seeks it in that which is in its essential nature precarious. He presumes upon the realization of conditions which are not intrinsic to him, or within his control. This happiness is subject to the law of uncertainty, to the qualification of an unyielding, mysterious *perhaps*. Here lurks the possibility of despair. Give a man the full satisfaction of his wishes and ambitions, and he deems himself happy; withdraw from him the smile of fortune's favor, and disappoint his expectation and his hope, and he will be plunged into despair. The shift from happiness to unhappiness in such a life is every moment imminent. And therefore its despair is latent even in its happiness, and discord lurks imminent in the soul's most beautiful music; its presence is masked only by a brutish self-satisfaction, the habit of thoughtlessness, breathless haste in trifling errands, and darkness in the soul's deepest ground, each and all miserable defenses indeed against the enemy within the gates.

A third consideration. Wealth and power and the like, even bodily health and beauty of person, are not in the strictest sense intrinsic values, but rather representative and comparative, conditional and hypothetical. Money is good — if I have learned how to use it; and so with power and influence, health and strength. But in themselves these things are abstract and neutral, and no man can truthfully say whether the acquirement of them in any individual case will work more good than harm. This is a consideration which applies to nearly every item of what we call progress. A new discovery or invention, like the printing press, promises radically to improve life, to secure for us a hitherto undreamed-of happiness and well-being. We hail it with enthusiasm as inaugurating a new era, and in the distance we descry the dawn of a millennial day. A century or so passes. What then? Why, all the old difficulties and problems, all the old dissatisfactions and complaints, the very difficulties and problems that were to be solved by the new invention, are seen to be still with us, having but slightly changed their outward form and habitat. In addition, the new improvement that was to usher in the millennium, is seen to be the source of so many and so serious abuses (consider the abuse of the printing press!) that the best minds of the race have to be concentrated upon the problem of finding a remedy for these abuses, and keeping them under some sort of control. And so also in the individual life. Every access of power and prosperity, and of outward comfort, brings with it its own griefs and dangers. Every such improvement is only potentially a good, as it is also potentially an evil. It is a mere quantity whose qualitative meaning is indeterminate, awaiting the seal of something else, something from within the soul itself, in order to determine its final significance for weal or woe, for happiness or unhappiness.

Lastly, it must be pointed out that the conditions of happiness as conceived in all such views of life, inevitably imply a privileged status for the happy individual. They rest upon differential capabilities and exceptionally fortunate circumstances. To choose them as the end and aim of life constitutes an injury to the mass of men who are not so privileged. This one thought alone is of so arresting a quality as to give the deepest concern to every man who has the least trace of human sympathy and human feeling. I hope I have a soul not entirely a stranger to happy admiration; I know I feel moved to bend low in respect before exceptional talent and performance, and that I am eager to honor greatness and genius wherever I have the gift to understand it. And I am not so unfeeling as to refuse a tribute of sympathetic joy to those who rejoice in fortune's favors and bask in the smiles of outward success. But as the fundamental source of inspiration of my life, I need something that is not exclusive and differential, but inclusive and universal. I require to drink from a spring at which all men may refresh themselves; I need an aim that reconciles me to high and low, rich and poor, cultured and uncultured, sophisticated and simple; to the countless generations of the past as well as to the men and women of the future. I need a spiritual bond that binds me to all human beings in a common understanding of that which is fundamental and essential to human life. To have my life and happiness in that which is inaccessible to the many or to the few, seems to me an act of treason to humanity, a cowardly and pusillanimous attack upon the brotherhood of man; for without the inner spiritual tie of an essential aim which all can reach and all can understand, the concept of the human race as a spiritual unity is destroyed, and nothing is left of mankind but a biological species, only slightly better equipped than the other animals to cope with the present state of their physical environment. The differences between man and man are indeed inseparable from this our imperfect temporal existence; but I cannot and will not believe that their development constitutes the perfection of life itself. Rather is this to be found in the discovery and expectation of something underlying and absolute, something that can be found by all who seek it in earnest, something to which our lives may give expression, subordinating to its unifying principle the infinite multitude of ends, reducing them to their own relative measure and proportion, and refusing to permit the unimportant to become important, the relative to become absolute. The possibility of making this discovery and of giving it expression is, so it seems to me, the fundamental meaning of life, the source of its dignity and worth. The happiness that is found with this discovery is not invidious and divisive, but unifying and reconciling; it does not abrogate the differences, but it destroys their power to wound and to harm, the fortunate through being puffed up in arrogance and pride, the unfortunate through being depressed in envy and disappointment. For this happiness is not denied to any man, no matter how insignificant and humble.

Our criticism has brought us to the threshold of an ethical view of life. That the essence of life and its happiness is to be sought in the moral consciousness alone is the conviction that animates this address, and gives it its reason for being. This view holds that the individual human self has an infinite worth, that the personality has an eternal validity, that the bringing of this validity to expression in the manifold relations and complications of life is the true task of the self, that this task gives to the individual's historical development an infinite significance, because it is a process through which the personality in its truth and depth comes to its own. " Find your self," says the moral consciousness; " reclaim it in its total and in so far unworthy submergence in relative ends; dare to think the nothingness, the hollowness, the relativity, the precariousness, the lack of intrinsic meaning of that which constitutes the entire realm of the external and the manifold; liberate yourself from slavery to finite ends; have the courage to substitute the one thing needful for the many things wished for, and perhaps desirable, making first things first, and all other things secondary — and you will find that these other things will be added unto you in the measure in which you require them and can use them as servants and ministers of your highest good."

So speaks the voice within us, a still small voice, a soft whisper easily overwhelmed by the noise and traffic of life, but a voice, nevertheless, which no one can permit to be silenced except at the cost of acquiring restlessness instead of peace, anxiety instead of trust and confidence, a distracted spirit instead of harmony with one's self. The moral spirit finds the meaning of life in choice. It finds it in that which proceeds from man and remains with him as his inner essence rather than in the accidents of circumstance and turns of external fortune. The individual has his end in himself. He is no mere instrument in the service of something external, nor is he the slave of some powerful master; nor of a class, a group, or party; nor of the state or nation; nor even of humanity itself, as an abstraction solely external to the individual. Essentially and absolutely he is an end; only accidentally and relatively is he a means. And this is true of the meanest wage slave, so called, in industry's impersonal machine — precisely as true of him as it is of the greatest genius or the most powerful ruler.

Is there anyone so little stout-hearted, so effeminately tender, so extravagantly in love with an illusory and arbitrary freedom, as to feel that the glorious promise of such a view of life is ruined, its majestic grandeur shriveled into cramped pettiness, because the task which it offers the individual is not only an invitation, but also an obligation as well? Shall we confess that we cannot endure this " Thou must " spoken to ourselves,[1] even when the voice proceeds from no external power but from our inmost self, there where the human strikes its roots into the divine? Truly, it is this " Thou must " that is the eternal guarantee of our calling, the savior of our hope, the inspirer of our energy, the preserver of our aim against the shiftings of feeling and the vicissitudes of circumstance. It steels the will and makes it fast; it gives courage to begin after failure; it is the triumph over despondency and despair. For duty is the eternal in a man, or that by which he lays hold of the eternal; and only through the eternal can a man become a con-

queror of the life of time. It is in the moral consciousness
that a man begins truly to sense the presence of God; and
every religion that has omitted the ethical is in so far a
misunderstanding of religion, reducing it to myth and
poetry, having significance only for the imagination, but
not for the whole nature of man as concrete reality. The
moral consciousness is a lamp, a wonderful lamp; but not
like the famous lamp of Aladdin,[2] which when rubbed had
the power to summon a spirit, a willing servant ready and
able to fulfill every wish. But whenever a human being
rubs the lamp of his moral consciousness with moral passion, a Spirit does appear. This Spirit is God, and the Spirit
is master and lord, and man becomes his servant. But this
service is man's true freedom, for a derivative spirit like
man, who certainly has not made himself, or given himself his own powers, cannot in truth impose upon himself
the law of his own being. It is in the " Thou must " of God
and man's " I can " that the divine image of God in human
life is contained, to which an ancient book refers when it
asserts that God made man in his own image. That is the
inner glory, the spiritual garb of man, which transcends
the wonderful raiment with which the Author of the universe has clothed the lilies of the field, raiment which in its
turn puts to shame the royal purple of Solomon. The lilies
of the field [3] cannot hear the voice of duty or obey its call;
hence they cannot bring their will into harmony with the
divine will. In the capacity to do this lies man's unique distinction among all creatures; here is his self, his independence, his glory and his crown.

I know that all men do not share this conviction. Youth
is often too sure of its future. The imagination paints the
vision of success and fortune in the rosiest tints; the sufferings and disappointments of which one hears are for youth

but the exception that proves the rule; the instinctive and blind faith of youth is in the relative happiness of some form of external success. Maturity, on the other hand, has often learned to be content with scraps and fragments, wretched crumbs saved out of the disasters on which its early hopes suffered shipwreck. Youth pursues an ideal that is illusory; age has learned, O wretched wisdom! to do without an ideal altogether. But the ideal is there, implanted in the heart and mind of man by his Maker, and no mirages of happiness or clouds of disappointment, not the stupor of habit or the frivolity of thoughtlessness, can entirely erase the sense of it from the depths of the soul. The present generation of men — particularly in the circles of the cultured and the sophisticated, those who are often called "intellectuals" and who perhaps also think of themselves as constituting a special class, characterized by a particularly acute awareness of life — the present generation exhibits in marked degree a loss of faith and enthusiasm, which it is pleased to call "disillusionment," and which perhaps also is disillusionment. They think of themselves, these moderns, as beset with despair;[4] the values that formerly seemed to be unquestionable have somehow gone dead, and many of them find nothing by which they are enabled to see life as dignified and serious. By and large, this despair is an aesthetic despair, an imperfect despair, which has not yet reached the ethical, or grasped the boundless meaning of the moral realm in its truth. Morality is for them not an infinite spontaneity, an inner life, an emancipation and an ennoblement of the self; it is for them mainly a system of conventions and traditional rules, an arbitrary burden imposed from without by social forces that have been outlived; or it is a mere device for reaching finite ends, whose worth has become doubtful. In so far as this despair is an aesthetic despair, it is all to the good; for this is the road which the spirit of man must take in order to find itself. Let us but learn to perceive that no differential talent, no privileged status, no fortunate eventuality, can at bottom be worth while as a consummation; that all such things are quite incapable of dignifying life; and when the misunderstandings with respect to the nature of a moral consciousness have been cleared away, the road will be open to the discovery of man as man. A preoccupation with the secondary thoughts and interests of life is always exhausting and trivializing, and in the end bewildering. Our true refreshment and invigoration will come through going back to the first and simplest thoughts, the primary and indispensable interests. We have too long lost ourselves in anxious considerations of what it may mean to be a shoe-maker or a philosopher, a poet or a millionaire; in order to find ourselves, it is needful that we concentrate our energies upon the infinitely significant problem of what it means simply to be a man, without any transiently qualifying adjectives. When Frederick the Great asked his Court preacher if he knew anything about the future life, the preacher answered, "Yes, Your Majesty, it is absolutely certain that in the future life Your Highness will not be king of Prussia." And so it is; we were men before we became whatever of relative value we became in life, and we shall doubtless be human beings long after what we thus became or acquired will have lost its significance for us. On the stage some actors have roles in which they are royal and important personages; others are simple folk, beggars, workingmen, and the like. But when the play is over and the curtain is rolled down, the actors cast aside their disguises, the differences vanish, and all are once more simply actors. So, when the play of life is over, and the curtain is rolled down upon the scene, the differences and relativities which have disguised the men and women who have taken part will vanish, and all will be simply human beings. But there is this difference between the actors of the stage and the actors of life. On the stage it is imperative that the illusion be maintained to the highest degree possible; an actor who plays the role of king as if he was an actor, or who too often reminds us that he is assuming a role, is precisely a poor actor. But on the stage of life, the reverse is the case. There it is the task, not to preserve, but to expose, the illusion; to win free from it while still retaining one's disguise. The disguising garment ought to flutter loosely about us, so loosely that the least wind of human feeling that blows may reveal the royal purple of humanity beneath. This revelation is the moral task; the moral consciousness is the consciousness of the dignity that invests human life when the personality has discovered itself, and is happy in the will to be itself.

Such is the view of life to which the present speaker is committed. He has sought to make it seem inviting, but not for a moment has he wished to deny that it sets a difficult task for him who would express it in the daily intercourse of life. Perhaps it has long since captured our imaginations; for it is no new gospel worked out to satisfy the imaginary requirements of the most recent fashions in human desire and feeling; on the contrary, it is an old, old view. But it is not enough that the truth of the significance inherent in having such a view of life should be grasped by the imagination, or by the elevated mood of a solemn hour; only the heart's profound movement, the will's decisive commitment,[5] can make that which is truth in general also a truth for me.

II

Progress in Religious Thought

This address was delivered originally in January, 1929, before the Minnesota Religious Workers' Conference held at the University, and was published in the University Bulletin, *Vol. 32, No. 6, February 12, 1929.*

WORDS AND PHRASES in common use tend markedly toward ambiguity. The thoughts and feelings that they purport to express have not always been subjected to an intellectual discipline capable of endowing them with that clarity, consistency, and precision which is the condition for a genuine understanding of oneself, or a mutual understanding with others; consequently we frequently have a meeting of minds on the basis of nothing more substantial than smooth and familiar phrases that fall trippingly from the tongue.

It seems to me that this danger is not wholly absent from the current use of the phrase that embodies the topic of my address. Progress is always relative to some sort of yardstick of change, some conception of a *terminus a quo* and a *terminus ad quem*. It implies the presence of a system of values and a scale of valuation. And since human life presents an extraordinary multiplicity, not to say confusion, of different and often contradictory values, it is natural that the word "progress" in its common use should be less a precise category of thought than a vague expression of complacent feeling, a turgid mood of self-congratulation in which the individual is far from being clear over precisely what it is that pleases him in the changes to which he attributes the eulogistic title of " progress."

I have therefore thought it best to deal with the topic which the managers of the conference have entrusted to me (a topic, by the way, not of my own choosing, and not entirely natural to my own habits of thought and speech) in a manner that may possibly disappoint your expectations. I am not unfamiliar with the ritual customary upon the occasions when progress happens to be the theme. The speaker is apt to place himself in an attitude presumably identical with the latest phase of dominant fashion in the world of thought. In the enthusiasm of the moment, this fashion becomes the eternal truth. Looking back upon the changes that come within the purview of his observation, he reads them all as so many stages through which mankind has had to pass to reach its present lofty height, necessary, indeed, as milestones of progress, but in no way to be compared with the excellency of the present attainment. And all the while it is as if soft music were insinuating into our souls pleasing variations of a theme which sounds something like this: " Every day, in every way, we grow better and better."

Pleasant and inspiring as this ritual is, it grieves me that I cannot upon this occasion perform it for your benefit. I feel a stiffness in my legs [6] and a lack of nimbleness in my wit which warn me of an incapacity for this performance that perhaps had better be openly avowed than inadvertently exposed. I cannot overcome a sense of embarrassment and difficulty when I face the latest developments of concurrent thought, due to the insidious reflection which will intrude, in spite of all my efforts to repress it — the thought, namely, that every error that history appears to have exposed was at some time or other the latest form of divine truth or the most perfect achievement of the human intellect. It is this thought that has always incapacitated me, and deprived me of the necessary agility, when faced with the task of gracefully identifying myself with the latest attitude, whether in philosophy or in religion.

For these and other reasons I shall not make any attempt, in this address, either to estimate the rate of progress possibly achieved in recent years within the field of religious thought, or to list the items of that progress, or to stir your enthusiasm with a vision of what the future may bring forth. I shall confine myself to the humbler task of calling attention to a few preliminary distinctions. In particular, I shall call your attention to an ambiguity in the phrase "religious thought" itself, and seek to show that it conceals at least two systems of valuation quite independent of, and incommensurable with, each other; and that these systems of valuation are the ruling principles of two entirely different concepts of progress.

Religious thought is either thought about religion and religious matters in general, or it is thought about anything — politics, the present task, myself, the world, my neighbors, and so forth — in so far as this thought is imbued by religious passion and dominated by religious categories. The significance of the distinction lies in the fact that thought about religion, in so far as it fulfills a cognitive function, must, in the first instance, be of so abstract and neutral a character as not to be religious at all in the sense of being actuated by a religious motivation. This does not mean that it is irreligious, but only that its purpose and place within the concrete personality, which alone can be religious or irreligious, is, in so far as such thought is abstractly intellectualistic, undefined and indeterminate. Thought about religion is exactly like thought about anything else in being in the first instance a tool, whose actual use for good or for evil is not predetermined. But the thought that surveys life and things in the light of religious values has abandoned this abstract attitude of impersonal neutrality and has become the reflective expression of a religious personality in the service of religious ends.

Thought always has a direct and immanent motivation, as well as a possible external teleology. The direct and immanent motivation is the desire to know, and this desire is satisfied when knowledge has been attained, quite irrespective of whether such knowledge has also been put to a satisfactory use. Hence it is quite possible to say that increase of knowledge means increase of sorrow, in spite of the fact that the ideal end of knowledge is doubtless to be found in solving human problems and thus banishing sorrow from the world. In its abstractly intellectual character thought about religion is 'impersonal. It is aloof and disinterested, moving on a neutral metaphysical plane which makes for cold clarity rather than warm enthusiasm. This impersonal vision may express itself directly, without bias or coloring, in which case it sounds like a voice from the clouds: or it may be incorporated into a more concrete personal attitude, and this personal attitude may be either religious or irreligious. The impersonal knowledge that illuminates the nature of religion in general, or of some religious category in particular, is something that both attitudes may have in common, just as attack and defense use the same geography, and wasters and savers rely on the same arithmetic. A philosophy of religion that had succeeded in attaining the maximum of metaphysical objectivity in its presentation might seem at one and the same time an attack and a defense of religion, depending on the attitude of the reader. The metaphysician says, " Such and such are the facts, ideas, and valuations that constitute religion; such and such are the varying types of the religious attitude." The religious man may share this knowledge. But in him it is not permitted to remain in a mood of metaphysical indifference; he adds, "Therefore I will embrace and follow this way of life with all my heart and soul." A consciously irreligious man may also share the same knowledge, but in him again the mood is transmuted into an active abhorrence; he says, "So and so it is, and hence I will have nothing to do with it." Pascal says that the Christian life is inseparable from suffering, and says it as a Christian; Feuerbach and Nietzsche say the same, but say it as an argument for its rejection as inhuman and pathological. Here is an instance of Christian and non-Christian thought sharing together a common core of thought about Christianity; in the same way religious and nonreligious thought may carry a common core of knowledge about religion.

There are those who believe that impersonal knowledge is the sole and adequate determinant of the human attitude. For them all radical differences between men are ultimately due to differences of knowledge; the hope of an eventual unanimity lies in the progress of science. Such is not the view of the present speaker — quite the contrary. I believe that knowledge is always fragmentary, and that any attempt to reach a total and conclusive view must frankly transcend knowledge and avow itself as an article of faith. Such a view will be a choice among alternatives, a subjective attitude in which the personality is revealed and expressed. We spend so much time in asking questions of life that we sometimes forget that life also asks questions of us, questions that we cannot help answering in one fashion or another. Religion is a subjective attitude, an individual choice of an interpretation of life involving the rejection of alternative interpretations, in which we give at our risk a definite answer to the question which confronts us daily: " What do you take to be the meaning of your existence and its activities? " And this answer is a passionate answer, an ardent interest, an enthusiasm of a specific sort, bearing within it the potentiality of a whole system of valuations.

Let me sketch, in three bold strokes, an outline of the religious attitude. In the first place it is not partial, relative, tentative, temporary, or experimental. The subordinate practical attitude of daily life may be so described, and cannot justly be otherwise entertained. But not so the deeper faith which underlies them all, and carries them forward, making us capable of enduring both their successes and their failures with a certain equanimity of temper. The religious attitude is a final commitment of the self, the assumption of a risk in which all is lost or all is gained. It is precisely this quality which is the source of its ennobling power, giving to even the most simple of men an air of distinction which is often lacking in the great.

The religious attitude is one that exalts the spirit of man above the things of the world. It seeks to make man the free master of such tools and instrumentalities as may be at his disposal. It seeks to make him free in having them and free also in not having them, when they are no longer at his disposal. He is in the world, and yet not of the world, convinced that the end of life lies in realizing the spirit of man as man, persuaded that every human being has his own goal in himself, and that this goal is essentially the same for all, the binding tie that links humanity in a brotherhood before God.

Religion is also convinced that suffering is an essential concomitant of human life,[7] essential not as a brute fact to be endured and minimized, but as an instrumentality of perfection to be welcomed and utilized. The religious teleology of suffering is grounded in the view that every human self stands in need of a transforming discipline. Pleasure is static, expressing a well-being that now already is; pain is dynamic, and in its religious uses is preparatory for a well-being that is not yet, a happiness of which the soul is not yet capable. The deliberate exposure of the soul to the transforming power of suffering, with a view to the perfecting of the human spirit, with all that it implies in the way of a transvaluation of the evaluations instinctive to mankind, is of the very heart of religion. Whatever beliefs may otherwise be held concerning God, the future life, and the soul, the absence of an acceptance of suffering as a radical ingredient of human life essential to a realization of its teleology, marks all such beliefs as nonreligious. It is not belief in a God that makes a view of life religious, but the presence in it of religious categories. Religion is *how* we believe in God, and *how* we take life as a consequence.

Thought that is imbued with these motives and their cognate implications, thought that seeks to assess the facts and circumstances of life in terms of such values, is religious thought in the second sense of the term. It is clear that progress in the one kind of thought is not necessarily progress in the other kind of thought. Each has its own scale and determinants of progress; the two scales are indeed not opposed to one another, but they are incommensurable, and there is no necessary or inevitable relation between them. Intellectual progress is compatible with moral and religious retrogression, as well as with moral and religious advance; and the converse relation holds equally true.

We have said that there are two different kinds of progress possible in connection with religious thought. There is the intellectual progress pertinent to thought about religion, and there is the religious progress pertinent to religious interpretations of the problem of living.

Progress in the former sense means first of all an increase in the scope of the relevant contributory knowledge. It means additions to our historical information, advances in the psychological, anthropological, and sociological sciences, a correction of errors formerly held, and an increasing accuracy in the prevailing methods of inquiry, as well as an enlargement of the available material. It means also an increase in the clarity and profundity of the interpretative ideas brought to bear upon this material, their greater internal consistency and an increase in their systematic connectedness with other ideas, a juster sense of proportion as between the parts of knowledge, an increased degree of emancipation from confusion and irrelevancies. In brief, intellectual progress in this field means a more intensive cultural sophistication with respect to religion, and a more extensive diffusion of such sophistication among the masses of mankind.

But how shall progress in the second, or distinctively religious, sense be evaluated? It is evident that the evaluation must either be in terms of values which are themselves posited by religion, or in terms of nonreligious values. If the nonreligious values are lower than the religious, and justly subordinated to these, then it is evidently nonsense to apply them in this connection, since the lower cannot justly be made the judge and standard of comparison for the higher. To recommend religion in terms of the service it may incidentally happen to render the subordinate interests of life is therefore indirectly to dethrone religion, and, in a sense, to betray it to its enemies, in so far as it demands to be the ruling passion. That religion is often a balance wheel in society, an amelioration of the bitterness of social conflicts, a conservative force that renders possession more secure, and lessens the difficulties of the art of government, may in some sense be true, and has been made the substance of such compliments as irreligious statesmen pay to the representatives of religious institutions. But these representatives would do well to look upon such compliments with suspicion, and perhaps even upon occasion to show sufficient confidence in their own cause to repudiate them as unconscious impertinences; for is it not effrontery for the lower to assume to patronize the higher?

Speaking for myself alone, I confess I know no higher standpoint from which to attain an estimate of the religious progress of religious thought than that which is immanent in the religious standpoint itself. Such progress will have to be measured in terms of the intensification and purification of the religious passion, the increasing domination by this passion of the judgments passed upon men and things, the increasing permeation by religion of the everyday relations of life, and an ever current renewal and deepening of the fundamental commitment of the self to the religious point of view.

To make these two concepts of progress more clear and distinct, I shall take up a few modern developments in the field of thought, as illustrative examples, asking how far they may be regarded as exhibiting one or another category of progress.

It is obvious that the last century has seen an enormous increase in knowledge concerning religious customs, rites, traditions, and institutions. The sheer mass of this more recent addition to our information is impressive; and an almost equally impressive fact is the extraordinary extent of participation in such knowledge on the part of others than scholars, scientists, and theologians. The quantity of reflection available to the average man on the subject of religion is unprecedented, and even a high-school student nowadays has a degree of sophistication with respect to it that makes it difficult for him to achieve a primitive emotional impression. Whether or not we are more religious than our ancestors is another question; but there can be no question that we make use of what would have seemed to them an astonishing amount of reflection and an extraordinary range of odds and ends of knowledge. The coming to a religious decision is now by a long and roundabout route, and the path is beset with a multitude of considerations of which our fathers were largely innocent.

The evidences of this increased reflection, the great number of books and articles dealing with religion appearing from the press annually, are not in themselves a necessary proof of a growing interest in religious matters, an interest that testifies to the vitality of the modern religious impulse. To draw this conclusion automatically would be to ignore the distinction between an intellectual curiosity and a religious interest. It would be to ignore the fact that the intellectual interest in a passion or a mode of life often manifests itself with increased intensity just as the passion or mode of life in question is about to lose its vitality as a present and challenging actuality, in order to be relegated to the limbo of the curiously interesting past. A happy lover rarely feels the need of a psychological theory of his passion, nor does he at once plunge into sociological studies dealing with the institution of marriage. But a frustrated individual, an unhappy lover, or one in whom the passion has begun to cool, may indeed often seek consolation or a new interest in the pursuit of scientific studies dealing with the waning phase of his life. Whether the present intellectual interest in religion is to be regarded in this light, I shall not venture to say; but the possibilty that such may be the case needs to be carefully considered if we are to avoid a serious misunderstanding of ourselves and of our times.

Another comment is perhaps of lesser importance. From the fact that the *quantity* of our reflection upon religious matters has enormously increased, it does not follow that the intellectual *quality* of our thought has been improved in an equal degree, nor even that the level formerly reached in this respect has been maintained. Certainly, now as always, a great deal of slipshod thinking upon religion sees the light. Much of what I am compelled by my duties as a student and teacher to read seems to me to bear the marks of a very distant acquaintance with the subject matter. A sympathetic insight into religious experience at close second hand is already rare enough to be remarkable; while I should scarcely know where to find an intellectually significant interpretation of the religious experience based upon a powerful and full-blooded religious passion in the writer himself. And a modern theologian, using modern tools of thought, comparable in intellectual distinction to Saint Augustine or Thomas Aquinas, if he were to arise among us, would doubtless make quite a different impression upon the mind from that produced by the many talented writers who at present attempt to satisfy our intellectual needs with respect to religion.

Be that as it may, it cannot be denied that all branches of science, including those parts of psychology and anthropology that pertain to religion, its history and its manifestations, have recorded marked advances, not only in the range of material made available, but also in the more important matter of accuracy and reliability. From the standpoint of science this constitutes progress; from the standpoint of religion the question of what progress has been registered is not so easily answered. The effort to assimilate modern knowledge to religious thought, and to deal reflectively rather than instinctively with this basic passion, has to a very considerable degree engrossed our attention. It would be surprising if, in addition to our undoubted gains, there may not also have been incurred some losses. Can we be sure that, in our effort to apprehend the religious experience through reflection, we have succeeded in maintaining vitally intact its power over the life undiminished, preserving its idiosyncrasy of form in the individual as a sign of the genuineness of its concrete assimilation? Can we boast that we have retained its essence whole and entire while translating it into the language of reflection, letting fall away only its irrelevant and accidental and nonreligious accretions? What has become, in all this intellectual process, of the *aggressiveness* natural to a faith that feels itself to be a victory over the world? Is not religion today on the defensive, at least in cultured circles? And what has become of the paradoxical enthusiasm which once had the boldness to embrace suffering as a gospel, and the consciousness of sin as the entrance to a new life? When rightly pondered, these are sobering questions, and capable of inducing a more critical frame of mind toward the conception of an unmixed " progress."

In any case, the intellectual progress in connection with religious phenomena — of which some moderns are so acutely aware that it almost tempts them to unseemly boasting whenever they have occasion to mention it — this intellectual progress becomes religious as well only when it is so used by the individual as to intensify religious passion and deepen its furrows in his life.

The newer knowledge enlarges enormously our conception of the vastness of the universe, and seems to place the little earth that man inhabits in an obscure and insignificant corner of it. Our solar system is only one of many such systems, say the astronomers, and their measurements of the interstellar spaces, replacing our customary units of distance by such extraordinary concepts as light-years, namely in order to make the numerical expressions manageable, almost take our breath away, if they do not paralyze the imagination altogether.

This alteration and extension of our scientific conceptions has been interpreted religiously. On the one hand, we are told that it mediates a more exalted notion of God, and thus intensifies the religious feeling. And, on the other hand, we are also told that it must necessarily minimize our sense of the importance of man, and render it impossible to view man as the chief object of God's concern.

It seems to me that both these interpretations suffer from a confusion of the categories. The infinite vastness of space is no measure either of the greatness of God or of the littleness of man, if man and God are to be viewed from the point of view of spirit. The true standard of God's greatness is his righteousness and his love; the true measure of comparison which exalts God in terms of spiritual values is the comparison between the human heart, which condemns itself, and the greatness of God's heart, which nevertheless forgives and pardons. And if man occupies but an infinitesimal fraction of the space in the universe, and if his abode is peripheral rather than central in it, what influence can this have upon a mind that is convinced, as the religious mind is convinced, that a single act of self-denial on the part of a single human being is in God's sight worth more than all the suns and moons and stars taken together?

The only way in which the progress of science, in the particular aspect under discussion, could essentially modify the moral and religious evaluations would be by tempting men to substitute for these valuations the values of a lower and incommensurable order; in which process it would not so much modify religious and ethicoreligious thought as destroy it.

Religion explains life teleologically, by assigning to it a purpose of a specific kind, and justifying life through the nature of that purpose and the conviction that it is possible of realization. On the other hand, the mechanical science of the nineteenth century found in the structural elements of the world, which were the chief objects of its inquiry, neither consciousness nor purpose, but a certain neutrality between good and evil, which it was in consequence tempted to ascribe to the universe concretely and as a whole. A more recent science has discovered new structural elements; and a mathematical philosophy has arisen that argues persuasively for what it calls an organic conception of the ultimate descriptive and explanatory units of the universe — and if organic, then also teleological.

Is this advanced phase of scientific and metaphysical thought to be counted as a strengthening of the religious interpretation of life? Superficially it would seem so, and yet I cannot bring myself to believe that the interests of religion have been especially furthered, even if the speculations of such men as Whitehead today should turn out to be the accepted scientific truth of tomorrow. For I believe the difficulty, in so far as there is a difficulty, to lie in an entirely different place, and to be of such a character that the progress of science is powerless to remove it.

That mechanical tools, machines, apparently dead and inert masses, and the like can be made to realize a human purpose (and perhaps also a divine one), is a fact with which man has been familiar ever since he began to use tools and invent machines. Taken singly, the elements of the universe need not be organic or teleological in character, in order that they should be susceptible to a combination into a whole which in its concrete totality has a purposeful character. So that this incommensurability which exists between the mechanical as such and the teleological as such is no necessary bar to their synthesis in a concrete unity.

The difficulty is elsewhere. For the purpose that religion posits as the justification of life is one that is as yet only in process of realization. And it is difficult to hold fast with assurance to an end not yet seen, a goal which does not yet exist. But this difficulty is inseparable from a human existence lived *sub specie temporis*. If the progress of science could abolish time, then it could also remove the difficulty; but it would then also destroy that essentially human feature of life which constitutes the challenge and the opportunity of religious faith, the faith that lays hold of the things not seen, and thereby overcomes the world and its vicissitudes. In so far, then, as this opportunity has an aspect that makes it also an obstacle and a difficulty, I am unable to see how any progress or mutation within the intellectual realm is at all likely to remove it. As long as there is a future that future will remain uncertain, and the uncertainty can be conquered only by the assurance of faith.

Biblical science has made great strides in the critical study of our religious documents, the testimonies handed down to us through the ages, recording the religious experiences and the religious convictions of bygone times. In so far as we now understand better the problems of their authorship, their date, their social environment, and their text, we can boast of having realized an intellectual advance. If this added and better knowledge concomitantly brings about a more effective use of the same documents for the enlightenment of the conscience, the intensification of the soul's ardor, and the communion of the individual with God, we have the right to speak of a religious advance as well. But if not, the intellectual advance in question is religiously indifferent, a mere relativity which in the last analysis neither adds to nor subtracts from the religious life. And if this new and interesting knowledge tempts us to substitute a scrutiny of the documents for a scrutiny of ourselves in the light of the documents, then its religious value will have to be reckoned as negative. For every divine word is a mirror; but an absorption in a study of the mirror as a glassy surface, no matter how entertaining, is not a use of it as a mirror. The extraordinary achievements of Biblical criticism in our day constitute a challenge to the religious consciousness in the sense that they create both a temptation to be overcome and a problem to be solved, and it is only our success in meeting the challenge that can count for religious progress.

Let me cite one last illustration. Within the field of Christian theology, scholars have made what seem to be important contributions to our understanding of the historical milieu of the Early Christian Church, and to the historical person of its Founder. Not that finality can ever be claimed for such researches, but our historical consciousness with respect to the early days of Christianity has doubtless been enriched and clarified. Here, at any rate, it is tempting to set down these scientific results as marks of religious progress. For is it not the ambition of every Christian to know his Master better? And is not such better knowledge a step which brings him nearer to his Lord?

Let us ponder this question for a moment.

The maximum result of the researches of the historians, the culmination of their most ambitious dreams, if they could be realized — what would the possession of these results yield us? The very most that they could do for us would be to place us at the standpoint occupied by historical contemporaries, and to give us the information that a zealous contemporary might have been able to collect and to check. To ask more of the historians than this would be to ask the impossible; to ask even so much is to ask what is impractical.

To be in effect a contemporary of Christ [8] — what is the religious value of such a situation? Would we then readily know what to think of him? Would his significance for our lives then be clear, without controversy? Would all Christological questions then settle themselves as a matter of course? Alas, we know indeed that it is not so. The religious problems concerning his person, and the significance of his teaching, were in the contemporary situation as critical and as disputable as in any subsequent generation. The essential religious point of view regarding the Founder of Christianity is that which regards his historical character and the historical detail as a " sign," revealing the intents and thoughts of the hearts of men by challenging them to an interpretation — an interpretation in which not historical accuracy is the deciding factor, but the needs and aspirations of the soul. Historical research is powerless to remove the difficulties of the Christian challenge, or to minimize the responsibilities of the individual with respect to that challenge. Before this phenomenon, and the testimonies that recall it to our minds, the generations are essentially equal. If any kind of progress had power to destroy this equality, it would also have the power to abolish Christianity.

Let these examples suffice to illustrate the theme of the present address, namely, the heterogeneity of religious progress and religious thinking with other kinds of progress and other kinds of thinking, even when the latter touches upon so-called religious subjects and hence tempts to a confusion.

The law of ethicoreligious progress differs essentially from the law of all other progress, whether material or intellectual.

With respect to material advances, each generation stands upon the shoulders of its predecessors, and begins its own progress where the last generation left off, utilizing its accumulation as social capital. Apart from convulsions that sweep whole civilizations root and branch, if such convulsions ever completely effect so radical a destruction, the discoveries and inventions which mark our progress need be effected only once. The way of the originator may be hard, but the way of his successor is relatively easy. It would be both foolish and futile to demand of each successive generation that it retrace the steps and assume the difficulties of the first inventors of those devices that have made life more comfortable and more complex. Such progress is cumulative, and we of a later age can enter into the inheritance of the past with only a fraction of the effort that the past itself had to put forth in order to secure the inheritance. And what is true of material progress is also true of intellectual and scientific progress, though not without certain qualifications to which we need not here advert.

But moral and religious progress does not follow this law. Because preceding generations have learned to love nobly and unselfishly, it does not follow that we can dispense with the major part of the discipline which they had to undergo, and begin where they left off. With respect to such a problem, each generation, and each individual in each generation, is compelled to begin at essentially the same place, namely, the beginning. No man can enter into the inheritance of a moral and religious hero without himself retracing essentially the same difficult steps that made the hero great. The way cannot be made either easier or shorter in the spiritual life, without rendering the values attained correspondingly cheaper and less significant. Here the price is always the same for the same; the progress of civilization and culture cannot modify the essential conditions of the moral and religious task that exists for every man. Ethicoreligious truth is not to be separated from the way of attaining it; here the truth is the Way and the Life. Any attempt to alter the way is therefore also an attempt to modify the truth. And it is as impossible to be born a Christian because one happens to be born in a Christian country, as it is impossible to be born thirty years old because the parents may happen to have attained that age.

This law is the secret of the essential unity of the human race, which is realized only in the ethicoreligious consciousness, and nowhere else.

But if this is the law of ethicoreligious progress, it is evident at once that it becomes very difficult, if not impossible, definitely to say whether the human race at any given time has actually registered such progress or not. For to determine this, one would have to have possession of the individual consciences of the members of the generations to be compared, and to understand them in all their concrete individuality, as only God can know them in his omniscience. For a historian or a philosopher to pretend to such knowledge is of course nonsense, a mere forgetfulness of essential human limitations, not better than any other kind of absent-mindedness.

I suppose that no age has been more concerned than our own with the concept of progress, and especially with the concept of progress as applied to the human race at large, as distinct from the individual man. And yet I ask to be permitted to express a doubt whether any human being has ever derived real light upon his individual task, or real strength for overcoming his individual difficulties, by permitting his imagination to be allured through the picture of some world progress he has permitted himself to entertain. For when we substitute for ethical self-contemplation the contemplation of the world process, or of humanity's progress, it becomes impossible to retain, pure and unmixed, the distinctively ethical point of view. We cannot see everything in such contemplation, only the outstanding facts; and the quantitative principle of selection which determines these outstanding facts nullifies the ethical significance of the resultant view. We may imagine that we see something ethical; in reality we see something heterogeneous with the ethical.

Man plays his role in life upon two stages at one and the same time. He plays a role in the world drama, and he plays a role before his own conscience. What part he plays in the world drama he cannot know, and the attempt to forecast his own historicity only enfeebles the vigor of his moral resolution upon the smaller stage, where he is his own spectator. The great drama is God's own spectacle; the little drama is man's most pressing business. It is here, and here alone, that he is able to measure the progress made in ethical and religious terms. This measurement is not essentially a matter of public interest, but concerns himself alone. All genuine ethical contemplation of life is self-contemplation. The contemplation of human history is not ethical contemplation, and the measurement of human progress is not essentially a measurement of that progress in ethical or religious terms.

III
Evolution and Life Values

This address was delivered originally on February 12, 1932, at the University of Minnesota, in a series sponsored by the Minnesota chapter of Sigma Xi, honorary scientific society, and was published in the Minnesota Alumni Weekly, *August, 1932.*

A LL HUMAN LIFE is a search for satisfactions, and the object of every such search is a real or imagined value. These values present an infinitely varied manifold. They differ from one another in a multitude of ways: in partial or universal accessibility, in turgid confusion or transparent clarity, in depth and intensity, in degree of permanence, in substantial worth. They range from the trivial and innocent pleasures of life, its private comforts and casual conveniences, to the ideal and more or less sharable satisfactions of contemplation and culture, the values of beauty and of art, of knowledge and of thought. They range from the ephemeral satisfactions derived from momentary absorption in things external to ourselves to the profounder joys deriving from the very roots of our being. They include the immediate satisfactions of the sensuous and vegetative life, the ensnaring and illusory objectives of blind passion, the phantasms of our daydreams, the mirages of hope, the transcendent aspirations of the spirit. They include the anarchic hosts of ungoverned promptings, and also aims so anchored in the distant future as to be capable of giving a direction to the whole of life, inspiring a devotion by virtue of which lesser values may be subordinated or resigned.

It does not come within the intended scope of this address to deal specifically with all these values. It is proposed instead to consider certain selected aspects of the scientific concept of evolution, and to ask what bearing they may have upon the needs and aspirations of the spiritual life, conceived as involving a special and distinct order of satisfactions. The broader theme suggested by the phrasing of our topic I ask you to regard merely as a convenient abbreviation, simultaneously serving the purpose of forestalling certain misunderstandings to which the more precise formulation is unfortunately subject. In view of the possibility of such misunderstanding, an attempt to make the meaning of this conception of a spiritual life more clear and explicit is evidently in order.

The life of the spirit is a form of human life dominated and unified by an idea. Human lives may and do degenerate into a kind of hand-to-mouth existence, devoid of persistent direction. But in spite of the obvious suggestions of a surface reading of experience, and in spite of the tragic failures marking the path taken by every life, a deeper insight and a bolder faith must insist that the way to a concentration of life about some fundamental principle is never entirely closed. A drifting, rambling, un-co-ordinated series of happenings, a random collection of shifting moods and reactions, devoid of every inner principle of unity and control, is a pitiful caricature of what human life can be and should be, a shabby counterfeit of that stamp of humanity which marks our distinctive worth. But given an idea capable of constituting its purpose and comprehending its meaning, then human life stands revealed as something nobler and stronger, having the stamp of character and the vigor of concentration. The personality receives a center, the dissipation of its energies in wasteful eccentricities is checked, and its life is molded into a concrete form through the presence and influence of a ruling passion. An idea acting as a pervasive, organizing principle, is thus the initial presupposition of the spiritual life.

A second qualification is required, in order to reach an ideal conception of the life of the spirit. Is the organizing idea intrinsic or extrinsic to the personality, essential or accidental? Is it relevant to the nature of the individual, or more or less foreign and arbitrary? Is it a harsh and cramping strait jacket for the self, or an emancipating and developing energy, an idea within which the personality moves freely and finds itself at home? Is it an impossible and fantastic dream, or is it the precise ideal required in order to explain and justify and transfigure the real individual? In reflection upon these and similar distinctions we find another presupposition of the life of the spirit, namely, that the idea that guides it and forms it must be an idea intrinsic to the essential nature of the personality.

A third qualification lies very near at hand, and is suggested by the preceding considerations. An organizing principle of the highest validity must have the power to elicit the total potential interest of the individual. An idea incapable of commanding the complete devotion of the self is *ipso facto* inadequate to the organization of its life as a whole. Only an idea of inexhaustible fullness and of infinite commensurability could serve this purpose. A finite idea may organize and transform a human life partially, but only an infinite idea can organize and transform it totally.

The pursuit of fame, the ambition of power, the desire of wealth, the purpose to realize some specific achievement in science or art, the will to attain a ripe old age — these and a hundred other ideas are capable of giving to the life that embraces them some degree of unity and direction. But it is not rational to permit such ideas to control life absolutely. Wholeheartedly and unreservedly to commit oneself to an idea that defines some merely finite goal is a sort of madness, and belongs to the pathology of the spiritual life. The supreme ruling passion of life must not be permitted to degenerate into the fanatical pursuit of a fixed idea. On the other hand, the submergence of the spirit of man in stupid torpor, its imprisonment in a trivial and self-complacent mediocrity, its anxious avoidance of intercourse with any idea that transcends the finitely calculable, is, in spite of its commonness, no less pathological than the wildest fanaticism. It is of the essence of the spirit to be awake; the spirit sleeps when man has no purpose to which he can yield an unreserved loyalty, no goal to which he can commit himself with his entire heart and soul.

The controlling influence of a unifying idea genuinely intrinsic to the personality, infinitely flexible in its relation to varying circumstances, inexhaustible in its significance, unlimited in its power to elicit and sustain the total potential interest of the individual — such is the principle which the present address takes as definitive of the life of the spirit.

It would unduly complicate our problem if we attempted here to describe and determine all the concrete forms of human life that might claim to embody the general principle thus formulated. At least two such forms are generally recognized, namely, the ethical and the ethicoreligious. It will be a convenient additional restriction of the scope of our address if we therefore define its problem as the relation between these two forms of human life and the concept of an evolutionary process in nature. And in order to make the statement of this theme as clear as possible, I will add a brief characterization of the two forms of life here indicated, in terms of a few traits that may serve to define them partly in their common, and partly in their separate, natures.

The essence of the ethical spirit is the identification of the meaning of life with the realization, by each individual as an individual, of his own true self, through a concrete historical process in which time plays a positive role. The self to be realized is conceived as given, and in so far as an unalterable necessity. But it is also conceived as a task, and in so far as an end for the life of freedom, the problem of its realization confronting the individual with the twin possibilities of success and failure. The synthesis of these two aspects of gift and task, of necessity and freedom, is what yields the sense of duty, the sense of an ethical obligation as constitutive of the essential form of the moral life. The duty of being and becoming one's own true self is thus the ultimate ethical duty, the source and fountainhead of all secondary and derivative duties. That the ethical life when so conceived embodies the principle in terms of which we have just defined the life of the spirit should be evident without further discussion.

The ethical life is the core of the religious life, but the latter is concretely qualified by means of an added determinant. The concept of the givenness of the self, and the sense of obligation attaching to its expression and realization, is in the religious life developed into a conscious emphasis upon the derivative nature of the human self. The self of man is not original, is not self-positing, is not self-existing. It derives from a power higher than itself; it cannot therefore find itself, or maintain harmonious relations with itself, without at the same time finding and expressing its fundamental relationship with the higher power from which it derives. If the ethical happiness of the individual lies in his being truly himself, his religious happiness lies in his being himself before God. The religious consciousness is the consciousness of the theological self; that is, of a self whose value and meaning is infinitely intensified by apprehending itself not only as standing in relation to a natural environment, or as having intercourse with a social environment of equals, or as a self related to itself, but as a self whose self-relationship is at the same time a God-relationship.

In view of the limitations inherent in an address, it might seem that I have dwelt disproportionately at length on one of the two terms of our problem; in view of the importance of clear conceptions in this connection, the characterization of spiritual values here offered is doubtless only too inadequate. Let us now turn to a consideration of the other term of the problem: the biological-scientific concept of evolution.

The idea that constitutes the central core of every evolutionary theory, the irreducible minimum of its logical content, is the idea of the mutability of species. According to this principle, the organic forms of living things are not absolutely invariant; under favorable conditions they are capable of such modification as may in time give rise to new species. The apparent rigidity of living forms dissolves upon a closer examination and a wider survey, leading to the conclusion that their fixity is limited, and relative to circumstances. A survey of the evidence comprehensive enough to include the facts of embryology, the data of experimental genetics, the paleontological material of the stratified portion of the earth's crust, and the known phenomena of geographical distribution, throws what appears to be new light on the entire field of biology. Investigators who have devoted their lives to the examination of such problems are with almost complete unanimity committed to the conclusion that specific organic forms are subject to change, in a manner and under conditions possible of verification, and in part even susceptible of experimental control.

A second idea usually identified with evolutionary theory is the principle that all living things are descended from a single relatively simple protoplasmic unit. This second idea, like any other idea attempting to solve the same historical problem, is inherently somewhat speculative; the evidence that can be brought to bear upon it, whether *pro* or *contra,* is of necessity indirect; its value as evidence depends upon complicated inferential considerations. Furthermore, the idea of a strict monistic origin for all forms of life is logically independent of the idea of the mutability of species; it is possible to deny the former while affirming the latter. Nevertheless, once granted the principle of mutability as established fact, the thought of a single origin for all forms of life is so irresistibly suggested to the mind, its illuminating and organizing power in relation to otherwise blind and incoherent data of natural history is so extraordinary, and its fruitfulness as a working hypothesis so demonstrably great, that it has become an integral part of the texture of modern biological science, pervading the organization of all its parts, coloring every theory and principle of explanation. Discovery of evidence that would compel the abandonment of this idea would *ipso facto* also force a revolutionary change in the entire logical structure of modern biology.

A third idea is so frequently associated with the concept of an evolutionary process that its omission from the present context would doubtless seem arbitrary and inexplicable. I refer to the view that inorganic phenomena are in so far continuous with organic phenomena that the origin of life from specific inorganic conditions is in principle explicable as a special exemplification of general law. This idea is not so much a part of the principle of biological evolution as it is a primary postulate of natural science; it deals with the presupposition within which biological science finds its problems. In the present state of scientific advancement it is a speculative conception. We are without concrete knowledge of the nature of the circumstances that might favorably mediate a transition from the nonliving to the living; the laws of such a change have not received specific formulation. This third idea has thus the present status of a hypothesis, a program for research and a problem for investigation; it is not yet a scientific theory whose concrete probability on the basis of available evidence can be gauged with any degree of accuracy.

The mutability of species, the monistic origin and consequent interrelatedness of all forms of life, the continuity of the transition between the inorganic and the organic in terms of natural law — these three ideas are separate and distinct; they do not stand or fall together. Nevertheless, I propose for our present purposes to treat them as a collective whole, and to refer to them as the principle of evolution. In a purely scientific inquiry it would of course be important not to lose sight of the differences between them. But here we are engaged in attempting to answer a different type of question, a question as to the bearing of these concepts upon certain values believed to be involved in human life. This question can be discussed hypothetically. *If* the principle of evolution as defined in terms of any or all of these ideas is valid, what consequences follow for the spiritual life of man? In the discussion of this question it will be realized that the differences of meaning and scientific status obtaining with respect to the three ideas we have distinguished are of no special significance for the elucidation of our own purely hypothetical, and therefore essentially logical, problem.

It will be seen that I do not propose to waste your time and mine in an attempt to demonstrate the truth or falsity of evolution. The communication of scientific evidence in all its inherent precision of thought and accuracy of statement is attended with such strict limitations and exacting conditions, that a quasi-popular lecture necessarily becomes a very dubious vehicle for the purpose. And the special problem of presenting the evidence in the light of which the validity of the theory of evolution must be judged is of so intricate and complicated a nature as scarcely to indicate an hour of more or less attentive listening as adequate to the purpose, but rather suggests years of intensive study on the part of specially gifted minds as the only road to a significantly independent judgment.

But even if the impropriety of attempting proof or disproof in an evening's address of so technical a scientific issue as is presented by evolution were not immediately apparent, it would still be wholly inappropriate for the present speaker to venture into this field, or to offer any sort of assurances respecting it. In what I have said concerning the scientific status of the principle of evolution and its component ideas, I have spoken simply as a reporter and a layman. In reference to these matters I formally disclaim the right to an independent or authoritative judgment. Such minor competence as might possibly be ascribed to me within the realm of thought pertains to a wholly different field of study. It is even essential, for an understanding of what I have to say, to remember that I do not speak in the role of a biologist, or of a student of natural science. I comment on certain logical questions connected with our topic in the character of a student of logic, but essentially I direct myself to the universally human question that our topic presents simply as an individual human being, interested in its solution precisely as every other human being is interested.

The sensible and intelligent layman will entertain a profound respect for the prevailing scientific conclusions of his age, appreciating the enormous labor of research and the distinguished talent of thought that has entered into their achievement. He will understand as a matter of course that no human science is infallible. He will realize that scientific generalizations having their roots in empirical or historical data have and can have no other validity than the validity of being consistent with the available evidence, and of explaining the known facts more completely than any available rival principle. The truth of such principles consists not in a demonstrated absolute certainty, but in a demonstrated relative probability. Logic and history unite in teaching the salutary lesson that all general conclusions with respect to the course of nature must be held subject to revision, and that no stage of scientific advancement can be regarded as final or conclusive. On the other hand, his respect for the principle of order in human life will also teach the layman that no revolutionary change in the canons of a science is ever likely to come about except as a consequence of extraordinary and specialized competence in its author. It is scarcely the part of wisdom to imagine that some more or less talented individual, consecrating the major portion of his time and energy to entirely different pursuits, casually dabbling with the problems of some special science in the leisured interstices of an otherwise busy life, will in this manner make himself competent to instruct the scholars whose entire lives are devoted to the science in question, or be able really to effect a genuine revolution in its intellectual structure. Over against every suggestion of some such miracle, one is prompted to remember the ironical comment of Socrates in a similar connection, that "the promise is so vast that a feeling of incredulity will creep in."

If the principle of evolution as here defined has any important bearing upon the problem of the nature and existence of spiritual values in human life, it seems evident that such bearing must come through an extension or interpretation carrying it beyond the sphere of its immediate application. The impulse to generalize an established principle is profoundly rooted in the nature of intelligence. It frequently leads to the discovery of new and important truth, and often throws light on hitherto obscure aspects of experience. Nevertheless, it is obvious that every such extension or interpretation is subject to its own special risks of error and confusion. A consequence that is psychologically suggested is not necessarily a consequence that may be logically deduced. The prestige that legitimately attaches to a principle in the sphere of its origin does not always belong to its analogue in another field, or to its generalization in a wider field. The popular and technical literature of evolution is crowded with analogues and generalizations of widely varying value, each of which raises new and distinct problems of interpretation and truth.

No generalization of the evolutionary principle is more commonly propounded than the sweeping assertion anciently ascribed to Heraclitus, that nothing is permanent, that everything existing is in constant process of change in all its aspects. More than thirty years ago this university sponsored a series of lectures on evolution, concerning which my most vivid memory is that each speaker prefaced his address by defining evolution as universal change.

Oddly enough, this particular generalization is often matched by an exactly contrary deduction, namely, that nothing really changes, and that every phase of the evolutionary process is at bottom identical with every other phase. Still more oddly, it is not unknown for both these deductions to be enunciated by the same thinker. The prevalence of universal change is thus affirmed almost in the same breath as the principle that later stages of an evolutionary process are to be understood exclusively in the light of the earlier stages, which evidently nullifies the reality of the transition from the one to the other. Or it is asserted by its hostile critics that if evolution be true, man can be nothing but a complicated amoeba. It seems to me that both these interpretations are the fruit of a too complete absorption in abstractly partial considerations. The one view neglects the continuity, the partial identity, in terms of which the change is explained; the other view stares so hard at this continuity that it becomes blind to the fact that any change at all has taken place. Philosophical generalizations of this character are therefore the expression of a sort of learned professorial absent-mindedness. But their presence in the popular consciousness as more or less confused interpretations of evolution makes it necessary for us to consider them in their bearings upon the spiritual life.

If nothing is permanent in nature or in human life, our highest aspirations and profoundest experiences must be dismissed as illusions. For all human life involves the attempt to use and to master the changing by means of an appeal to the relatively or absolutely permanent, and the degree in which this holds true of an individual is a measure of his human significance. The sailor seeks to conquer the shifting seas by a glimpse of the starry heavens; the wise and prudent tell us to overcome the fears and apprehensions of a period of economic adversity by attending to the permanent underlying resources of wealth, and the persistent springs of energy and enterprise. The ethical individual conquers the discouragement or despair induced by the vicissitudes of life, or generated by the passing of the glory of the outer man, because he has found the way to the inner and incorruptible self. The religious man finds his way through the shifting sands of life guided and impelled by the thought of an unfathomable and unchanging love, the same yesterday, today, and forever, in which there is neither variableness nor shadow that is cast by turning.

Does the scientific validity of the principle of evolution mean that all this is necessarily false? Such an inference cannot be consistently urged. For the science of biology, like every other science, is itself an expression within the intellectual realm of precisely this human need to master the changing in terms of the permanent. Evolution is not only an assertion of the existence of certain kinds of change, but also a program for their explanation. This program is not yet completely realized, and it is possible that it never will be completely realized. The question of defining and measuring the factors of organic evolution, of determining how much weight should be assigned to sexual selection, to use and disuse, to body cells and germ cells, to climate and other environmental features, to gradual variations slowly accumulated, to sudden changes appearing at auspicious crises, to competition for the means of subsistence, to natural selection — these and many other similar questions are still in abeyance. The prevalence of differences of opinion respecting them has sometimes been interpreted as incipient or actual abandonment by the scientific community of the principle of evolution itself. This misunderstanding rests on the confusion with which we are here dealing, namely, the failure to distinguish between the changes affirmed by the general principle of evolution, and the concrete formulation of the constant laws in terms of which the changes in question require to be understood. Since science necessarily presupposes the possibility of an explanation as a motive underlying its activities of research, it follows that science itself demands the existence of some identity in the process of change, something permanent in the natural order. For science to abandon this faith in the face of discouragements arising from the incompleteness of the evidence, the fragmentariness of human experience, the possibility of human error, would be tantamount to a suicidal denial of its own essential nature. The pursuit of science is indeed a special form of practical life, and in this aspect it manifests precisely the same formal structure as every other practical activity: it is an attempt to use and master the changing in the light of the permanent. It is therefore a self-contradiction to call upon science to testify to the absolute instability of all things; in a world of such instability science could not hope to realize its aims.

All consciously planned forms of human effort, including the scientific, the ethical, and the religious, involve a faith in the permanent and an attempt to establish contact with it. This formal resemblance is of course not tantamount to concrete identity. Each form of faith must make its own way in the world, and win its own victories against its own specific obstacles. Religious faith is quite capable of standing on its own feet; the flourishing business of manufacturing scientific crutches for its support is one of the most stupid of all human follies. But whatever may be the motives that lead men to doubt or reject the religious thought that the temporal order in which change abides has its ultimate ground in an eternal order, it is clear that these motives cannot possibly derive support or confirmation from the discovery of hitherto unsuspected forms of variation in the temporal order, nor from the correlative efforts to find an explanation of these variations. No inference can legitimately be drawn from the principle of evolution that would destroy the possibility of finding an anchorage for the hope by which the spirit lives — the eternal meaning and ultimate justification of human life.

The appeal to the evolutionary process for the purpose of justifying a total rejection of anything permanent or universal in experience is nevertheless a minor misunderstanding, if we measure its importance by its popular appeal. The contrary misinterpretation is more generally prevalent, and masquerades under a greater variety of forms. The law of any process or event is always some identity of relation which it exemplifies. Whoever fixes his attention solely upon this law may therefore readily be persuaded that any explanation of a change cancels its reality. It is this paradoxical conviction, confused as it appears when thus baldly stated, which underlies the widely expressed opinion that if we once find an explanation of the origin of life, or of consciousness, or of man, this discovery would tend to destroy the reality of the supposed differences between the living and the lifeless, the conscious and the unconscious, the specific human dignities on the one hand and the subordinate values of animal instinct and intelligence on the other. And although this opinion has no more solid foundation than the one-sided absorption of the intelligence in a partial aspect of its problem, it is nevertheless widely accepted as valid both by friends and foes of the evolutionary principle. From such absent-mindedness the only rescue lies in a return to common sense. It should be possible even for a very learned man ultimately to recapture the naïve insight that water remains water after we have explained it in terms of hydrogen and oxygen, and that table salt does not lose its distinctive properties when it is chemically explained in terms of a metallic element and a poisonous gas. Qualitative changes in the natural realm are surely not destroyed by the quantitative identities which preserve for them a measure of continuity.

The reality and importance of the apparent qualitative differences which nature presents, and the genuineness of its phenomenal transitions, is in every specific case a question of fact, and of the standards of value we bring to bear upon the appreciation of the facts. It has nothing whatever to do with the presence or absence of a continuity yielding a basis for scientific explanation. The only primary evidence for the worth of the values intrinsic to human life lies in man's experience of himself. The circumstances of his origin, the numerous organic structures and functions which he possesses in common with the brutes, the vastness of astronomical or geological time as compared with the brief period of human history, the immensity of space and its innumerable hosts as contrasted with the local insignificance of the earthly center of human habitation — these considerations are one and all utterly irrelevant and extrinsic when the problem is to evaluate the dignity of human life. The proof of every pudding is in the eating; the proof of the ideal potentialities that ethics and religion ascribe to human nature, the test of the validity of the demands that in consequence they make upon it, is inherent in the depth of the enthusiasm they inspire, the loyalties they evoke, and the transformations they effect in the conduct of life. The plausible appeal with which even the flimsiest of arguments are invested when we consider such questions is merely a proof of the thoughtless frivolity with which we so often approach the problem of our ideal potentialities.

To deny the reality of change is to deny the reality of the historical process in which the individual finds the ethical opportunity to realize himself. It is to deny the genuineness of the victory by which the individual succeeds in making of time an ally instead of an enemy. It is indeed to deny the very existence of man as an individual, by virtue of denying the reality of the acts through which his individuality constitutes itself. In short, it is an attack upon all the ethical values of the spirit, a nullification of the life of freedom and responsibility. To deny the reality of change is also to attack the religious individual at the very core of his being; for the essence of religion is consciously to submit oneself to a radical process of transformation. The religious spirit thirsts for the redintegration of the personality in the forgiveness of sins as the one thing needful, thirsts and hungers for it more than the natural man thirsts for water and hungers for bread. This consciousness is the consciousness of a change more profound and significant than any other within the compass of human experience, a change whose meaning and value are inexhaustible. Hence it is that both ethics and religion, and all the spiritual interests of man, unite with logic and common sense in protesting that interpretation of the evolutionary process that would make its continuity and scientific explicability tantamount to its nonexistence as a real process of change, a process in which new phenomena actually appear.

When we have once dismissed from our minds the baseless fear that the admission of a continuity between man and the rest of nature is tantamount to a denial of any difference between them, we may without prejudice yield ourselves to a consideration of the bonds of kinship and resemblance which link us to nature both in its living and its nonliving forms. If there is any humiliation in the linkage, no mere denial of a specific hereditary descent from lower forms will save us from it: the actual resemblances and identities of structure and function are there for all to see, quite irrespective of any theory of evolution. The aesthetic protest against some sort of human kinship with the ape or the amoeba has no deeper ground than an idiosyncrasy of feeling, a lack of clarity of conception, a silly vanity as foreign to the spirit of religion as it is foreign to a more rational and cultivated aesthetic sensibility. This vanity is certainly not rooted in the religious consciousness. Does not the Apostle Paul say that the whole creation groans and travails until now, waiting for the deliverance of the sons of God, which certainly assumes a real if limited fellowship between man and nature, and shows no slightest sign of horror at the thought of a relationship. The sentiment expressed by the apostle evidently breathes a different spiritual atmosphere from that which finds expression in the defiant current repudiations of relationship, assuming to represent religious feeling. It seems to me that it would be a reflection not unworthy of a religious personality to consider that if an infinite mind has condescended to include the monkey in his scheme of creation, man, who boasts that he derives from the same ultimate source, might tolerate the thought of such degree of likeness and kinship as observation and research may disclose.

Let me recapitulate the heads of the foregoing argument. All interpretations of evolution that proceed from the principle of an antithesis between change and continuity, conceiving the latter as virtual identity, are in effect destructive of the values of the spiritual life. This holds true of them whether they stress change on the one hand or continuity on the other as evolution's essential meaning. The more sober and responsible interpretation, which affirms both change and continuity as correlative aspects of an evolutionary process, has no such application to the spiritual life, but leaves the problem of its values to be decided by intrinsic evidence. In so far as we accept the latter interpretation we are relieved of a disturbing obsession, and are free to face the question of the values of life without pseudo-scientific prejudice; the spiritual climate is not affected by either the acceptance or the rejection of a technical scientific theory.

The considerations already discussed have been highly abstract and general. I now proceed to certain ideas of a more limited application, ideas that purport to interpret the spiritual life in the light of evolutionary conceptions. The first of these ideas raises no question of change or continuity in general, but affirms a specific kind of continuity in the natural order as affecting the life of the spirit. It finds in the brute ancestry of man an explanation and a palliative for moral evil. Man is conceived as staggering under an enormous burden of ancestral brutishness; his sin is an inheritance from which the individual may hope to be relieved only through the gradual progress of the human race as a whole. It seems to me that this explanation suffers under the disability of taking its start from a misunderstanding of that which it proposes to explain. Moral evil is the pathology of the spirit, not to be identified with either the sensuous or the instinctive inheritance. The bestiality that is sin is not found in beasts; the brutishness that is the attempted self-destruction of the spirit is not a characteristic of the brutes. Moral evil is not to be identified with the promptings of the senses or the stirrings of flesh and blood as these are in themselves; its connection with these things is wholly indirect. It is rather to be identified with the refusal of the spirit to take up its proper functions of government and control, its craven consent to the rule of flesh and blood in a context that demands their subservience. The possibility of moral evil is a strict correlate of the possibility of moral good, so that both come into existence together; they are antitheses for the will, not stages in an evolutionary process. The ethical maturity of the individual is marked by the coming into being for his consciousness of the absolute distinction between good and evil, not as an object of historical contemplation, but as irreconcilable terms of an altogether present alternative.

There is another view that also interprets the evolutionary process as presenting a moral continuity. It seeks to find a moral pattern in those abstract biological processes that are present in both human and nonhuman life. The shallow optimism that in pursuing this will-o'-the-wisp rejoices in an illusory success is of the same intellectual caliber as the affected pessimism that despairs over its failure. Nature yields wonders enough to satisfy the contemplative mind, without also demanding that ants and spiders and squirrels and pitcher plants should satisfy a human ideal of social fellowship, and express in their behavior an ethical consciousness with which they are not verifiably endowed. The imputation of moral guilt to an animal nature "red in tooth and claw" seems to me a wholly overstrained interpretation of essentially nonmoral phenomena. And the attempts often made to justify the passions of war, the ambitions of conquest, the unscrupulosity of greed, the blindness of egotistic desire, by a reference to the phenomena accompanying the struggle for existence on nonhuman levels of life, as if these phenomena were the proper source of a moral standard for the life of man, constitute by the very futility of their appeal to the incommensurable an involuntary confession — a confession that human ruthlessness is wanting in intrinsic justifiability.

The principle of evolution is sometimes identified with a law of universal progress. It is supposed to testify to the presence in nature of an irresistible trend, a force making for the realization of ever higher values, in the cosmos, in the social structure, in the individual man. This thought is supposed to strengthen and encourage the individual in his spiritual strivings; as a matter of fact it is as likely to lull him into a dangerous and stupefying slumber. For it is capable of suggesting that progress in the realization of the good consists in drifting down the stream of time, that being born in the twentieth century is a moral virtue instead of a moral opportunity of a specific nature. And it further suggests that the measure of the difference between good and evil is to be found at the poles of a process so vast in its scope and so complicated in its details that the tiny fractional deviation in either direction that any individual human life may present becomes a vanishing infinitesimal invisibility, submerged and forgotten in the irresistible forward march of the whole.

The idea of a law of progress is, however, not an integral part of the principle of evolution, certainly not in the sense of an irresistible force directed toward a specific end. The conception of such a law involves a confusion between two very different things: the possibility of a certain concrete event, or series of events, whose realization is dependent on circumstances, and the notion of a fundamental law as a scientific principle of explanation. A fundamental law of nature is never, as such, a directed force; gravitation is quite indifferent to the balloon's going up or coming down, and is exemplified equally in the safe progress of the steady pedestrian and the dangerous antics of a car guided only by a drunken driver. The laws of evolution, whatever they may be, so long as they really are laws in the sense of scientific explanatory principles, will, in analogy with all the other laws of nature, be abstract and neutral entities, perfectly compatible with a concrete movement in any one of many different directions. The concrete event is the vehicle of whatever values may be involved, and this event is always a product of both law and circumstance, neither of which factors is derivable from the other.

When we speak of progress in connection with biological evolution, we usually mean a change from the relatively simple to the relatively complex, from the loosely organized to the organization that is more closely knit. That the history of living things discloses what seems to be a major trend in this direction over those periods of geological time for which we have interpretable evidence cannot be denied. But the simultaneous indefinite persistence of living forms presenting an essentially unmodified type of structure is also an undeniable fact. Nor are instances of the opposite process of degeneration and simplification unknown to biology. All these facts taken together clearly dispose of the loose talk about an irresistible trend in any given direction as a fundamental law eternally imposing itself upon phenomena. The same looseness of interpretation clusters about the scientific conception of natural selection, rhetorically phrased as " the survival of the fittest." The literal meaning of this phrase is the prosaic tautology that those survive who happen to be capable of surviving under the given circumstances. That these surviving forms should also be the best and fittest as judged by any given ideal standard of value is no part of the sober meaning of the phrase, but a confused extraneous interpolation. The vast variety of the existing, and hence at least temporarily surviving, forms of life is indeed such as to arouse the deepest wonder and admiration. But clarity of thought requires that this fact should be set down as belonging in the category of uncovenanted mercies; no principle is known that could reduce this precarious historical fact to an absolute necessity, a mere matter of course whose continued and even intensified existence constitutes an inevitable logical consequence of the laws of nature.

To speak of a law of progress, or of a necessary law of universal progress, involves the logical confusion that has just been expounded. But to speak of an evolutionary law of progress guaranteeing the security and ultimate realization of the values of the spiritual life involves an additional and still more profound confusion, a confusion of values. It fails to note that the biological scale which measures degrees and differences of organization is not continuous with the ethical disjunction between good and evil. The ethical spirit is jealous of the qualitative distinctness of its own values; it refuses to be cajoled or flattered into merging them with the essentially quantitative distinctions which play the decisive role in the biological scale. The ethical or ethicoreligious individual has his life in the decisive qualitative disjunction between good and evil. To attempt to incorporate this distinction in a quantitative-aesthetic series of biological values such as enter into the notion of evolutionary progress, to regard the ethical values as continuous with the values of this order, is profoundly to emasculate their meaning. Such an interpretation enervates the passion by which the individual maintains himself in the ethical disjunction and its qualitatively unique distinction from all other things; it quenches the ardor and relaxes the vigor of the spirit's enthusiasm.

The interpretation of evolution here in question fails to

preserve a necessary and proper distinction between the corporate history of the race and the personal history of the individual. Hence, of course, it fails also to distinguish between the values germane to each. Let the cosmogonist, if he can, envisage a goal for the cosmos; let the historian of civilization picture the end that fixes the direction taken by the progress of the race. In any event, the values whose realization marks the stages of this advance will not be the same values as those that mark the ethical success or failure of the individual life. Every individual, even the humblest, has a twofold existence. He belongs in greater or less degree to a public order of things, whose constitution and course is not merely the product of the voluntary deeds for which the individuals are responsible. His role in this public order is determined by a texture of conditions that he can make neither completely transparent to his consciousness nor completely subordinate to his will. The most loyal devotion to the good, the most hardened persistence in evil, are alike impotent to determine the particular historical significance that a subsequent contemplation of this public order will ascribe to him. The values disclosed by a survey of this order are the values of what we call social evolution. They are one and all abstract and quantitatively relative. This is not because the more concrete and qualitative values are not in a certain sense present in the historical process, but because despite their presence the eye of the observer cannot see them here, or extricate them from their social and public context. The human observer lacks the medium that alone would enable him to understand them, namely, the conscience-relationship of each individual with himself and with God. To say that the history of the world is the judgment of mankind is to forget this inevitable human limitation, and to confuse an imaginative projection of the ethical in oneself with an objective verification of the ethical outside oneself. No human being who writes the story of the progress of mankind will ever succeed in writing that story in terms of essentially ethical values; he will perforce have to content himself with what he can see, and this will be something abstract: aesthetic or ethicoaesthetic, quantitative, and relative.

But each individual, even the greatest, has a personal and private history that belongs essentially to himself alone. It is here that the ethical and ethicoreligious values clearly reveal themselves; here the life of freedom comes into its own. The ethical and religious values of the personal life are concrete and individual. The absolute distinction between good and evil which eludes the most faithful biographer, and altogether drops out of sight in the evolutionary process, has here its roots and its fruition. The objective historian finds only relative differences. But whoever loses his sensitiveness for the absolute disjunction in the subjective life faces moral dissolution. The elasticity and vigor of the will in keeping this disjunction alive is the health of the personality; without this the self has lost its savor, and is fit only to be " cast out and trodden under foot of men." The cosmic processes of universal history have their own categories and their own significance for those who think themselves capable of reading their meaning; without disputing the value of any scholarly speculation in this field, it nevertheless remains everlastingly true that a different meaning governs the individual's own private history. Here there is an issue that cannot be compromised; here the notion of *both* this *and* that points the way to destruction, while *either-or* is the key to heaven.

The confused and spineless optimism that finds a pseudo-spiritual encouragement in a supposed necessary law of evolutionary progress is of little or no worth in facing the real difficulties of life. There is only one sphere in which the virtue and power of the ethical and ethicoreligious values can be studied with profit, and that is the sphere of the individual life of the individual self. Here there is no cosmic law that safeguards the self against the possibility of failure. The confidence that in this sphere sustains the ardor of the spirit is quite otherwise founded. It is a treasure achieved and possessed in awe and fear and trembling. This faith rises to full and normal vigor in the very midst of an enveloping sense of the insecurity of existence. The consciousness of the possibility of failure is not its foe, but its friend. For the secret of the negative in life is that it guarantees the genuineness of the corresponding positive; the uncertainties of existence keep the spirit awake and its lamps burning.

There remains to be considered an interpretation of the principle of evolution that plays a large part in the popular consciousness, although it has little or no standing in scholarly circles, being based on a confusion of ideas readily apparent to reflection. There are those who find in the concept of evolution, not to say in the very word, an ultimate explanation of the existence of man; and, in the last analysis, a ground for the being of the entire evolving universe. For such minds evolution is the creative energy that brings all things forth from the womb of chaos; it is the guide and determiner of progress, the principle of realization of all values. Viewed in this light, evolution comes to mean the replacement of a religious idea by a scientific idea, setting science and religion into antithetical opposition. The discovery of the evolutionary idea makes impossible and superfluous that reference of himself to God which to the religious man is the very core of his being. Such an interpretation is avowed by combatants on both sides of the struggle, a struggle that pretends to draw a line of battle between God and evolution, and asks whether man comes from God or from the gorilla. A little reflection should suffice to show that this supposed antithesis is false.

In the universe of human thought there are many distinct kinds of explanation, each having its own specific clarifying office, each ministering to its own specific human need. We understand a thing when we know the purpose it subserves, when we know the mechanism of its action, when we know the agent responsible for its being. These different sorts of explanation are incommensurable with one another; the discovery of one does not make the search for the others superfluous; there can be no internal logical contradiction between them. Natural science is chiefly devoted to a search for the mechanism of events, and in so far as the evolutionary idea is a principle of natural science, and includes formulas of explanation conceived in the spirit of natural science, such explanation is bound to be mechanical in the broad sense of the word. But what is a mechanical explanation? Leaving aside certain controversies irrelevant to the present issue, we may say that a mechanical explanation of an event or phenomenon is attained as a result of analyzing it into its constituent circumstances, and discovering the universal relations, called laws of nature, in which these circumstances stand. All the factors of such an explanation are either general or particular constituents of the thing explained. A mechanical cause is a circumstance viewed in the light of the specific relation in which it stands, a relation that is called a law because it is precise and repeated elsewhere. Such causes are so far from explaining the coming into existence of the phenomena of which they form a part that they contrariwise presuppose such existence as given. Hence, it is clear that a mechanical explanation does not even raise the question of a productive or creative energy that would account for the being of the natural order; it yields formal structure, not authorship. What clarity of thought is there in saying that the parts of a thing are the forces that have brought it into existence? The notion that evolution is a productive energy, accountable for the coming into existence of life or man or civilization or religion or anything else whatever, is an unscientific confusion, the unimaginative misunderstanding of a rhetorical figure. And what holds true of the principle of evolution also holds true of any and every other law of natural science.

The reflection by which the religious man refers himself to God lies in a different logical dimension from that occupied by scientific explanations. The religious man knows himself as clearly not the original author of his own existence, and as clearly not the power that maintains him in existence. He sees no convincing reason to believe that the natural order of which he forms a part is more self-existent than himself. He finds himself compelled by the experiences of his life and the promptings of his nature to raise the very simple human question of the whence and whither of his existence. He seeks an answer that shall bring him into relations with the roots of his being, that shall justify his life by assigning to it a more than transient meaning and furnish him with a goal with the power to enlist all his energies. In this connection he is not directly concerned with the scientific search for circumstances and laws, but rather with a primal energy from which both laws and circumstances spring, an energy with which his spirit can find communion, his mind understanding. To make communion possible the energy in question must be immanent in the natural order; and yet it must also be transcendent of it, as being in every moment the ground of its existence. It is a simple and inevitable consequence of the religious consciousness of dependence, to believe that if God withdrew his hand for so much as the smallest fraction of a second, the entire universe in time and space would instantly dissolve into nothingness.

The possibility of such an explanation is the problem and province of the religious life. It does not come within the scope of this address to estimate the strength of the considerations, for and against, that pertain to its solution; our task will be achieved if we have shown that the principle of evolution is not itself either a positive or a negative solution of the religious problem, but merely an extraneous consideration. The religious problem is most clearly put and most significantly answered on the basis of those features of experience to which all have equal access. It is not a matter of scholarship or of trained authorities and technical specialists. It is every man's question, and its answer is peculiarly relevant to every man's experience. Neither the existence of temporary or permanent gaps in the tissue of scientific explanations nor the specific nature of this or that explanatory theory has anything essential to contribute to the religious problem. If the hand of God is to be seen only where science has failed to find a texture of continuity, whether in connection with the origin of life, or of consciousness, or of man, then the religious value of the God-idea disappears; for in that case it is shown to be incommensurable with the everyday detail of human life. And to find a God in the electron that did not reveal himself in the atom, to find in organic conceptions a religious evidence absent from the realm of the inorganic, to hail the quantum theory and to be depressed by the relativity theory, or vice versa — all such anxious scanning of the scientific horizon for proof or disproof of the validity of the religious attitude is a ridiculous inconsequence.

If there is any differential status between one human being and another with respect to the solution of the religious problem, it is certainly not based upon that superiority in scholarship which distinguishes the scientist. To offer such scholarship as mediator between God and man is so ludicrous a misunderstanding as to drown the respect and honor which otherwise rightly belongs to it in a flood of laughter from the very depths of existence. The impressiveness of any man's opinion on religious matters is directly proportionate to the depth of his human pathos, not at all to the extent of his technical learning. The strength and quality of his enthusiasm, the ardor of his spirit, the depth of his earnestness, the human intensity of his life — such are the only relevant guarantees any individual can offer to enforce respect for his attitude in matters of religion. And it is a common experience that these human qualities are as likely to be found in the kitchen as in the parlor, in the cottage of the humble laborer as often as in the professorial chair.

The aesthetic emotion of wonder and the ethical passion for a highest good constitute man's twofold sensibility for the divine. The emotion of wonder is first stirred by the contemplation of the aesthetic values everywhere revealed in nature and in life. In the appreciative consciousness for which these values exist it is as if they constituted a language in which mind speaks to mind, and spirit betokens itself to spirit. The forked flashings of the lightning, the rolling voices of the thunder, the majesty of the mountains, the vast expanse of the sea in calm and its terrible energy in storm, the sublimities of the starry heavens, the immensities of the interstellar spaces, the enormous periods of astronomic and geologic time, the infinite complexity of the smallest cell, the presence of law and structure in the least as well as in the greatest, the mathematical precision of nature's fundamental relations, the boundless variety of organic forms, the ingenuities of adaptation, the fertility of inventiveness shown in adjusting means to ends, the seeing blindness of instincts, beauty of crystal and rose and human form, of sunsets and fair fields, the miracle of consciousness, the profundities of social life, the dawn of the spirit — what soul so dead as not to be stirred by all this to admiration and awe!

Science and philosophy and religious reflection may each in its own way begin with wonder; but does not science end by abolishing it? Here we find the final interpretation of the principle of evolution with which our address will attempt to deal, the idea, namely, that in its capacity as measuring an advance in the powers of scientific explanation it cuts the ground from under the religious reflection that is rooted in wonder and awe. Does not every completed explanation reduce the explained phenomenon to a simple matter of course? What do we have our scientists and philosophers for, says Shakespeare, if not to make wonderful and miraculous things seem ordinary and commonplace? In these and similar questions we have an apparent intellectual paradox, and it will be worth our while to pause a moment over an attempt to discover its source.

The analysis of a phenomenon into its elementary factors, an analysis that discloses the terms in which its scientific explanation is formulated, is checked and verified when the corresponding intellectual synthesis gives us back the whole from which we started. If the sense of wonder seeks to find sustenance in the contemplation of this synthesis, it is cheated; for what is there that is wonderful in the fact that the terms of a correct explanation together suffice to account for the whole? It is neither more nor less than a mere logical tautology to affirm that a phenomenon analyzed is identical with the same phenomenon unanalyzed. It is in this sense only that science abolishes wonder, and makes everything that exists seem a matter of course; in the sense, namely, of furnishing us with a new intellectual object, or rather relation: the terms of its explanations, when compared with the phenomenon to be explained, exhibit the self-identity of the identical. This self-identity is certainly no miracle; but it does not follow in the least that the existence of the wonder has become any less wonderful than it was before being explained. The fading of wonder from the mind which sometimes accompanies the process of explanation is thus due to its misdirection: the attempt to focus upon a necessary logical relation instead of upon the existence of the value that in the first instance stirs it to life.

When the thinker comes to himself, and succeeds in liberating his reflection from its imprisonment in a partial aspect of the fact, the progress of science provides only new and greater wonders. But the values that excite this emotion also stir the mind to the apprehension of an ideal, the ideal perfection of completely and universally realized values. This aesthetic idealism is doomed to defeat; its imaginatively expanded demands are realized neither in nature nor in art. The sadness of the imperfect, of withered grass and fading flower, of maladjustment and apparent waste, of death and decay, descends upon the soul. That the aesthetic teleology of nature and of the outer man is and remains imperfect is no learned discovery; it is as obvious as the world about us and the sky above. This imperfect teleology has its part to play in the development of the spirit, but to seek in it a logical demonstration for the existence of God is a pedantic misunderstanding. Its very imperfection marks the necessity of a transition, for it is only in the ethical that there is to be found a transparent revelation of the divine. In this sphere also wonder waits: a deeper wonder, in which the individual confronts God himself rather than his gifts; an amazement so profound that every suggestion of an imperfectly realized ideal is excluded.

We have in the course of this address canvassed five or six different interpretations of the evolutionary principle, interpretations that seem to give it an influence upon the foundations of the ethical or the religious life. The principle that has suggested itself everywhere in the discussion is the principle of the heterogeneity of the concepts of scientific research with the categories of value that dominate the spiritual life. The present speaker cannot subscribe to the assertion that science and religion are only different languages expressive of the same reality. On the contrary, he believes that, whatever the language in which we formulate them, the human experiences for which these words stand grow out of different needs and embody different principles.

That science and religion lack the factor of identity that would enable them either to confirm or to contradict or to replace one another is a thought that can claim neither originality nor profundity. Nevertheless, it does not irk me to repeat it, for I believe it to be as true as it is trite. In a totally different sense they may indeed become rivals — rivals for the major attention and interest of the human mind. Religion demands the place of a ruling passion, and science may in some minds become such a dominant interest. Is science, or its fruits, capable of constituting a highest good? The millennium has often been proclaimed as the certain fruit of invention or discovery, and as often disappointed expectation. The best minds of the race have constantly to devote themselves to the task of eradicating the evils that the misuse of knowledge brings into the world. Let me, therefore, at the end, express the personal conviction that it is only for the religious man that all things work together for good — science and art, sorrow and joy, success and frustration, life and death. And if this be true, it follows clearly that it is he alone who is wise.

IV

Functions of Intelligence

This address was delivered originally on May 9, 1934, at the University of Minnesota Recognition Day exercises (a tribute to seniors who had gained recognition in various ways), and was published in Minnesota Chats *for May, 1934.*

IT IS PROPOSED in this address to deal with intelligence in a broad and liberal spirit, including within the scope of this term all its genuine forms and manifestations. We are to consider, indeed, those narrowly technical expressions of intelligence that meet us in academic scholarship: literary, historical, philosophical, and scientific; but also its less formal, if not less genuine, nonacademic expressions, those that meet us so often in daily life and are evinced by all sorts and conditions of men. And the attempt will be made to deal with these various expressions of intelligence from a variety of viewpoints, both technical and nontechnical.

It is hoped that we shall be able to speak of intelligence intelligently. Pascal once complained that few know how to speak of modesty modestly, of skepticism skeptically, or of religion religiously; i.e., few men understand how to reduplicate the content of their thought artistically in the form. We confront the danger that we should speak about intelligence in a stupid or unintelligent manner. But, in order to avoid this danger, it is necessary among other things to understand how to view intelligence with flexible minds, with minds not limited to a single habitual groove of thought; we need emancipation from such slavery, that we may enjoy and use the freedom of a variety of points of view.

And such a variety presents itself in connection with intelligence. There is, for example, the biological-scientific point of view, which stresses the survival value of intelligence; there is the closely allied individual-practical point of view, which lays stress upon the idea that knowledge is power in the hands of the individual, in competition with other individuals, and as control over the forces of nature; there is the aesthetic-intellectual point of view, which looks on intelligence and its fruits as an enrichment of life, valuable for its own sake, quite apart from biological or other consequences arising in the battle of life; and finally there is the ethical point of view, which looks upon intelligence as something to be used and directed, devoted to high and humane causes, and through such devotion comes to be a real and genuine good.

None of these points of view is rationally treated as exclusive of the rest, nor is any one of them all-sufficient for an intelligent understanding of intelligence; for this there is needed a synthesis of standpoints. Nor can any one of them be so regarded as fundamental that the others should be derivable from it, and thus stand revealed as secondary manifestations of a single fundamental category. Particularly must I beg to emphasize, as necessary to the understanding of the present address, and as a conviction of the speaker fundamental to his entire philosophy of life, that the ethical cannot be derived from the biological-scientific.

A scientific age, or rather an age that has accustomed itself to identify wisdom with science, especially natural science, has shown its partial want of intelligence by making the categories and working ideas of natural science intellectually absolute. It has attempted to usurp for such ideas a practical monopoly of the field of significant thought. This is a misunderstanding that has had costly consequences. Among other such consequences it has come about that many well-meaning but not clear-thinking persons have tried to derive the ethical concepts from those ideas that dominate the biological-scientific realm; in this process they necessarily adjust both sets of ideas in order to bring about a seeming accommodation. Man is indeed part of nature, but this does not mean that he is a *mere* reduplication of nonhuman nature, and that he has nothing essential that is peculiar to himself. That which is distinctively human is as real and as genuine and as natural to him as that which he shares with the rest of the living and nonliving world. To think otherwise is to make a fetish of an abstraction, and to cut oneself off from any communion with, or foundation in, a sound human common sense.

The ethical motivations in human life are the most characteristically human features of that life, things that no man will validly discover anywhere except within himself, when he yields himself, namely, to the ethical passion that is his essential birthright. And why should man so assiduously and avidly search the phenomena of a nonhuman nature to find an example or warrant for the ethical outside himself? Has he no proper pride or certain confidence in his specifically human dignity? Must he hesitate to obey the voice of duty within, the still small voice that comes from the very depths of his being, unless he can prove to his own satisfaction that stars and suns, ants and cockroaches, microbes and mollusks and monkeys, also own the sway of the same ethical ideas, and exhibit a mode of existence that is moral in the human sense of the word? Is not nonhuman nature sufficiently worthy and beautiful and interesting as pure physicobiological phenomenon, manifesting and exemplifying a group of natural laws which are for cold contemplation ethically neutral, and for reasonable contemplation rightly so neutral — is not this glory enough for nature outside man? Or must we confusedly and mystically impute to that part of nature which is external to man and his developed or undeveloped potentialities a moral law and standard of action that it does not reveal when considered in the light of a reasonable and enlightened common sense?

Morality is no crippled invalid, unable to walk or stand on its own feet, except through the help of crutches furnished by dint of a false interpretation of the meanings and principles of natural science. Whoever has once laid hold of the ethical in its ideality and inwardness, whoever has had his eyes opened to behold its boundless infinitude, and has had his entire being ennobled by the purifying sway of its all-engrossing and passionate enthusiasm, will no more ask for such external supports than the ideal lover will ask for a scientific justification and certification of his love before he dares to yield himself to it; for both the lover and the ethicist have that within them which is more to them than all science, past or present or future, however valuable this science may otherwise be to them and however much they may appreciate it and use it. When the ethical is truly present in a man, so that it constitutes his ruling passion, it stands as nothing else in all the world squarely on its own feet; it earns its own way in life, and is no Lazarus begging a few crumbs from a rich man's table. For whose sake do we then indulge ourselves in the circle-squaring nonsense of a pseudobiological and pseudoethical confusion of ideas? The biological and the ethical are not opposed, but neither are they identical or commensurable; the mistaken attempt to make them such either confuses biology by importing into it ideas that it cannot use and cannot assimilate or emasculates ethics by depriving it of its distinctive impulse and force; or it does both of these things at one and the same time.

After this long, but by no means entirely irrelevant digression, it behooves us to move more swiftly toward our goal. Fortunately, the main outlines of a biological point of view are necessarily so familiar to the members of an institution of learning, of higher learning, devoted to pure and applied science as related to some of the basic industries and occupations of human life, that a mere mention of these categories should suffice to point our moral and adorn our tale.

For biology, intelligence is one tool among many, a weapon useful in the struggle for existence. It gives an increased survival value to the biological behavior-patterns, and finds in this fact its explanation and its justification. Just as sight may, from the point of view of biology and biological psychology, be regarded as anticipatory touch, exhibiting most of the values of touch without incurring its risks and dangers, so intelligence may be regarded as an anticipatory confrontation of reality, an experience before experience, an experiential preparedness for experience. How necessary to man is such anticipation! When the sailor faces the angry seas, when the night and the clouds blot out his ordinary marks of reckoning, when reality preaches emphatically the urgent need for wise and immediate action, when the urgency of the need makes the breath come short and the pulse beat wild — is it then the proper time to acquire the science and the art of navigation? Hence we have the gift of thought, which makes in a sense the absent to be present, and helps us bind the past to the present for the sake of the future. Hence also education, with its seemingly superfluous wealth of knowledge and ideas, with its inexhaustible representation of possibilities not yet realized, and perhaps never to be realized; a wealth not immediately needed, nor usable, but nevertheless both immediately interesting and valuable as a happy exercise for the developing mind, and in the long run certain to be both useful and necessary, sometime, somewhere, and to someone, we may not yet know whom. Man is thus equipped with that which makes this comparative physical insignificance no essential handicap. He becomes capable of fashioning tools to give him a longer reach than any conceivable lengthened arm could yield; to give him those seven-league boots, or rather those wings of transportation, that are the wonders of our modern world; to give him a power of which strength of muscle and of limb is but a faint and imperfect adumbration.

Nevertheless, we may need to be reminded that this life-serving teleology of the intelligence is not absolutely effective value. There are handicaps, some of them actual in the world about us, some of them merely conceivable as possible, that man's intelligence, or perhaps any thinkable human intelligence, may be quite unable to overcome. How should our present equipment of intelligence be counted able to overcome the threat of destruction, to all that live on the surface of the earth, presented by a colliding comet or star? How overcome the threat to our existence presented by a radical though not impossible climatic change, making those organisms we now call lower most fitted to survive in the new conditions? Man, who proudly calls himself lord of creation, and perhaps in some sense of the word may really be such, has lived upon the earth only a small, not to say infinitesimal, fraction of the period allotted to much less developed organisms; these *may* possibly be here when man is utterly gone, despite his superior equipment. Nothing in physical or biological science can guarantee us against such a contingency. There are situations possible in which no conceivable intelligence, short of absolute and creative power, would avail to man. The survival value of intelligence to the individual man and to the *genus homo* is real and enormous, but it is not absolute.

Whoever knows the causes of things has power to produce or prevent their effects, says that preacher of the scientific method, Francis Bacon; his aphorism that "knowledge is power" has passed into the common stock of the world's wisdom. It is quite needless to elaborate on this commonplace; but it may be useful to note a few modifications and qualifications of the thought. Intelligence is not only knowledge; it is also grasp. It is not only information; it is also clarity and needful abstractness of conception. Abstractness in thought is the subjective side of a properly analyzed fact or object of experience. For experience does not teach its most significant lessons immediately and upon its surface, so that he who runs may read; instead, nature loves to hide, and he who seeks the gold of useful truth must dig much earth and yet find very little gold, as was remarked of old by Heraclitus of Ephesus. The prima-facie values of observation and experience can rarely be generalized so as to furnish guidance for the future; this requires curious and shrewd and fortunately apt analyses, and for such analyses the abstract idea is the only available form of apprehension. There is an abstract intelligence that we call pedantic in its awkward absent-mindedness; it is at home in the realm of the abstract and universal, but quite at a loss in the realm of the particular and the concrete. Real intelligence is at the same time both concrete and abstract; for it the road is always open between the observed concrete particular and the conceived abstraction, so selected as to be relevant and fruitful. Genuine intelligence travels this road with equal ease in both directions — from the particular to the universal and from the universal back to the particular again; by which process the particular is illuminated and made ready to be understood. The most liberal conception of intelligence is that it is the control of experience by means of ideas. The quality and power of such intelligence depends on not less than two separate factors: the depth and scope of experience on the one hand, and the precision and sweep and absoluteness of our ideas on the other.

Shall we again remind ourselves that human intelligence, however great its development, is not equivalent to absolute power? We may soon learn to understand the immediate and ultimate causes of the production of earthquakes; but does it necessarily follow that we shall in consequence be able to prevent or control them? When biologists have thoroughly learned to understand the nature of the transition from the inorganic to the organic, it does not quite follow, or follow as a matter of course, that we shall at once produce living organisms in our laboratories. Possibly we may, and possibly we may not; it is at any rate conceivable that the necessary conditions will be beyond our control; or that they have existed only once in the world's history, or at any rate only in the past. That the world has a history means just this, that the past is never in all respects wholly and completely reinstated. But let us descend to lesser things. Who has not often had reason to take note, that the innocent of experience and the limited of intelligence *sometimes* come out best in the conflicts of life, while the sophisticated and the clever often make of their multifarious reflection a snare for their own feet, like a snarl of string which impedes and delays the footsteps of the hurrying. Intelligence is a wonderful instrument which can never be sufficiently admired; nevertheless, by itself it cannot solve the deepest and most pressing of the problems of human life. The English nurse,[9] the patriotic heroine of the Allied side in World War [I], is said to have remarked when, clear-eyed and resolute, she faced death, " Patriotism is not enough." And as with patriotism, so also with intelligence. There is required, in addition, a certain health and soundness of soul, an integrity of the personality, which the Greeks called wisdom, namely, the knowledge of how to use knowledge and power and all other goods — a wisdom that is therefore not identical with knowledge or science or philosophy in its ordinary and direct sense. This is that same health which religion conceives of as *faith* — a something that does not indeed control the vicissitudes of life, but that nevertheless succeeds in turning them to a good account, whether they be in themselves joyous or grievous. Without this health in the soul, the most exact and comprehensive science or the most profound and precisely conceived philosophy is but an extraordinarily sharp instrument placed in the hands of children or irresponsibles or fools. Who that is but a little more than thirty years old has not seen how the finest instrumentalities of civilization, the most effective tools of science, have been used by the most advanced nations of the world so as to bring civilization itself to the verge of destruction? And who that is but a little open-eyed today does not see that preparations are feverishly being made for a possible repetition of this major catastrophe, with still more effective instruments and with still greater hope of success — for the completeness of the contemplated destruction? Verily, neither science nor philosophy nor intelligence as commonly understood is enough by itself to solve the problems of human life.

Intelligence is at one and the same time a simplification and a complication of life. It is a simplification in that the control of an indefinite multitude of facts and considerations and experiences by means of some appropriate general idea reduces life's apparent and surface complexity to something that makes a synoptic view possible, and brings some semblance of order into its primeval chaos. But it is also a complication, since it makes possible an infinitely richer variety of response, of discrimination, of consciousness, and of understanding. This enrichment may be regarded as itself the chief of life's values, the crown and summit of the whole; it is so regarded from the aesthetic standpoint which would make intelligence an end in itself, its own sufficient justification, and the justification besides of whatever else there is in life that serves as its condition and necessary concomitant.

What American youth has not read Emerson, and learned from him that there is a view that makes thought as such the significant goal of life, refusing to consider it merely or mainly as a means to further or prolong existence? "We do not think in order that we may act," says the poet philosopher of Concord, "but we act in order that we may think." And Emerson is not alone in this conviction. In his treatise *The Value of Science,* the French mathematician and physicist Poincaré gives expression to the thought that we do not properly pursue science for the sake of food and drink merely, or for the sake of all sorts of instruments and machines to make our lives more secure and comfortable and easy; but we apply science to invention of such things in order that we may have more leisure to pursue science. Science and intelligence, thus conceived, become both means and goal, but essentially goal. They are thus ends valuable in themselves, having their chief purpose intrinsic to their exercise, not things externally motivated in their heterogeneous consequences. It cannot be denied that intelligence tends to make life more rich and significant, even when it does not make it longer and more secure. "Better fifty years of Europe than a cycle of Cathay." [10] Aristotle thought that human life and its happiness culminated in the pure pleasures of a disinterested reflection. To behold the thoughts grow out of and into one another; to inspect the delicate network of their invisible but none the less real and knowable logical organization; to achieve the enduring satisfaction of an intelligent and crystal-clear understanding; to know, and again to know *that* one knows and *how* one knows — who that has but slightly and intermittently tasted of these joys can think of them except as in the highest rank of human goods? The Greeks deemed these satisfactions to be divine, and Aristotle conceived of the blessed life of the gods as consisting exclusively in reflective self-contemplation, no higher object for their science and philosophy being thinkable.

Such felicity is the accompaniment of an abstract and disinterested reflection, in an environment that does not urgently press for the use of thought in action, and where no external or internal imperfection disturbs the peace of the speculative thinker. When thinking is impressed with a concrete responsibility and urgency, however, when problems of an actual and not merely formal order loudly call for solution at its hands, then thought is also charged with an interest that is passionate; the thinker is no longer wholly objective or disinterested; his thinking is impressed with a subjective purpose and aim. Under such circumstances the fruits of intelligence are not always sweet, and knowledge is not always the bearer of a pure and unalloyed happiness.

> " A sad self-knowledge, withering, fell
> Upon the soul of Uriel," [11]

is the half-concealed testimony of Emerson concerning himself. The German proverb makes it a universal principle: " *Wissen heisst Leiden.*" And the Hebrew sage speaks out to the same effect: " He that increaseth knowledge increaseth sorrow." When we consider these more or less obvious lessons from the life of thought, we need not be slow to recognize that a view that justifies life solely through the fruits of thought is too abstract a conception to suit the exigencies of a concrete human mode of existence which shuns the ivory tower as a cowardly evasion.

From the viewpoint of an ethical mode of evaluation, intelligence is, like all the other relative values of life, something that needs to be justified by being saved to good and noble uses. It enriches the personality quantitatively, and gives it a more translucent and definite possession of its inheritance in the world and in itself; but the qualitative significance of this enriched personality in terms of ethical good and evil is otherwise determined. When man learns that he must declare and prove himself by the use that he makes of those gifts with which he finds himself endowed, whatever be the road along which those gifts have come to him, then and not before does the ethical life begin; he ceases to be a child, and awakes to the status and dignity of manhood. For this mature view of life, the worth of intelligence is not an independently existing fact, assured to us through the objective physicochemical and biological processes, to be discovered, catalogued, and explained by scientists and philosophers, or celebrated in verse and form and color and story by poets and artists; it is rather a crucial problem for the life of freedom, an issue of success or failure for the individual, a task to be accomplished and an ideal to be realized, through the ethical devotion by which " man the master " is transformed into " man the servant."

The high priests of the modern business and professional world have well-nigh succeeded in ruining the beautiful word " service." In the jargon of the day, service is that for which we expect and receive the more liberal and ample forms of immediate reward. In the nobler lexicon of ethics, whoever proposes to render real and genuine service to any part of this imperfect world must expect in one way or another to pay for the privilege. I begrudge none of my student auditors the honors or rewards they will receive for services rendered, either to scholarship or to their associates or to themselves. But I covet for you, in a period of your lives when your increasing maturity will put you under increasing responsibilities — I covet for you then a higher form of honor, the proudest badge of nobility that human life affords, namely, the honor of bearing scars which tell of wounds received in the service of noble and humane causes, perhaps in the service of the truth itself. Such wounds are not for the moment pleasant; but in retrospect, in the perspective of the entire life, they are the source of man's only lasting happiness, the springs of his profoundest joy. It is for this reason that all genuinely good men are lovers of memory — and of eternity, which is the true memory of one's life, grasped in its essential significance. Such wounds are indeed the only passports into a higher world, the only passports exhibiting a valid countersignature; they are certificates of citizenship in the kingdom of the spirit. When intelligence is made to serve such ends, it is approved and justified, and enters as an ingredient into man's highest good. Such, at any rate, is the testimony borne by the ethical spirit.

V

Objective Uncertainty and Human Faith

*This was the president's address, delivered in December,
1927, before the Western Division of the American Philosophical Association, at the University of Chicago, and was
published in* The Philosophical Review, *Vol. XXXVII, No. 5.*

WHEN those whose lives are devoted to a more or less
successful courtship of philosophy come together for
the purpose of mutually correcting one another's errors,
sharing one another's insights, and kindling one another's
enthusiasms, the satisfaction they feel in these activities and
enjoyments is not infrequently marred by the intrusion of
a disturbing reflection. Their attention is often called to the
fact that the subjects chosen for discussion at these gather-
ings are for the most part such as to seem quite inaccessible
to the majority of men, and the terminology in use such as
to be intelligible only to those who have undergone a long
process of initiation. The great public can take little interest
in our proceedings, except in so far as the strangeness of
our jargon furnishes substance for its laughter.

An ambitious philosophy, one conscious of a mission with
respect to the world at large, addressing itself not only to
initiates but also to the plain man, the man unadorned
with the trappings of an academic reflection, must necessarily view this situation in a mood of protest. There is indeed a more modest form of philosophy, for which the
circumstance cited has another significance. This philos-

ophy is content to satisfy a need in the individual thinker, a need which he shares with relatively few of his fellow men, however deep-seated the need may be in him. It sees in the prosecution of philosophical inquiries an attempt to realize a genuine but relative good, relative not only in the economy of human society at large but also in the life of the thinker himself. The more ambitious philosophy has another consciousness of its significance. It claims universal and decisive importance, and is not content with assignment to a limited sphere in the lives of a limited few.

A philosophy of this kind faces a difficult dilemma. If the plain man is saved by philosophy, he must be saved either by one that he understands or by one that he does not understand. In the latter case his thinking has to be done for him on the principle of vicariousness. The philosopher becomes an authority, and the rest of mankind are asked to believe in him; in this faith they are saved. This is hard for modernists, seeing that we have such good modern authority for the dogma that the day of authority is past. In any case, the imagined situation is not one in which any genuine thinker is likely to feel comfortable. It doubtless makes him happy to share his insights; but it could scarcely occur to him, qua thinker, to ask for faith in himself or his results. The attitude of requiring faith is foreign to the atmosphere in which the thinker works, and quite irrelevant to his function in society. The thinker represents reflection; and authority and reflection are discrete and incommensurable factors in human life.

The more ambitious philosophy has therefore no other recourse than to formulate its processes and results so as to make them seem capable of a universal communicability. In its maximum of communicability philosophy attains the dignity of news, and its secrets are made commensurable for headlines. It is necessary on this view that all men become philosophers, since to be excluded from philosophy is to be excluded from salvation. Philosophy is often said to be the means through which the individual may realize an inner harmony of knowledge, passions, and will, a moving equilibrium of all his powers. If this be true, then it seems imperative that philosophy should not remain alien to anyone who is human enough to have this human problem set him as his chief task in life. For who would willingly entertain the view that what is essential to the good life should be inaccessible to the mass of men? Complacently to accept such a view — is it not to make oneself inhuman? And to seek with all the energy of one's heart and mind to find another explanation of life — is this not to prove oneself in so far possessed of humanity in thought and feeling?

I do not know whether the world is destined sometime to see the dawn of a day in which all men will stand revealed as philosophers, as Christianity teaches that all men ought to be priests. The years I have spent in attempting to make philosophy intelligible to college students have not made me oversanguine of such hopes. Not that my enthusiasm as a teacher has been chilled — quite the contrary — but I have been forced many times to acknowledge that there seem to be human beings so constituted by nature that philosophy is not essential to their peace. I am free to admit that the more primitively original expressions of thought in philosophers of the highest rank have a universality of appeal that the more trivial renderings at second hand, the translations and commentaries of pedagogues and other middlemen, fail to achieve. But in spite of all that may truthfully be urged in this direction, it still seems safe to admit that a talent for philosophy is a differential talent, and that the service of philosophy is an aristocratic privilege. It shares with all such privileges the obligation of paying its debt to humanity by understanding itself in a spirit of reconciliation with the common life, accepting its own perfection as something less and other than the perfection of human life itself. For the courtship of philosophy is not likely to be a hopeful enterprise unless it is predicated upon the possession of a somewhat rare and specialized talent, early opportunities in a favorable environment, a scholar's leisure, and an enthusiast's devotion.

The truth of this seems so obvious that I am afraid that I have convicted myself of banality in giving it expression, following the suggestions of a feeling that it might be suitable, on this holiday occasion, when the temptation to magnify our office lies so near at hand, to bring to your attention this reminder of its truth and possible significance. But if it is true, then philosophy has an interest in clarifying its relations with the common life, and it should be concerned to seek its own humanization along a pathway that is not impenetrable. In this view philosophy cannot be the absolute, nor man's point of contact with the absolute; it is a relativity among other relativities, although no thoughtful man could possibly assign it a place among the meanest. Like wealth and power, like beauty and fame, it is the possession of the few; the many are excluded from an intelligent appropriation of its values, not through any fault of their own, but by force of circumstance and nature's law. Philosophy satisfies a need that the individual feels in proportion as he is born a thinker; this need stirs the minds of most men only slightly and transiently. Not every man is fitted by nature to carry the burden of a philosopher's reflection, and not every man is equipped to think the thoughts of a philosopher after him.

But though it may be erroneous to think of every man as potentially a philosopher, and futile to demand of him a realization of that which is not potentially present, it is surely right to think of every philosopher as potentially a man. There is a view of life that demands of him, as of all men, that his deepest interest be focused upon the realization of this potentiality. The Greek skeptic, professing a philosophy that sought a radical transformation of human nature, after a pattern believed to be more rational than the simply human pattern, frankly admitted that even a skeptical philosopher was also sometimes a man, though by an unfortunate and exceptional relapse. But the more modest species of philosophy, in whose name I here diffidently and haltingly attempt to speak, will urge this fact with boldness and confidence, and embrace it with enthusiasm, seeking to become increasingly conscious of the claims of that which is universally human. The professor of such a philosophy will seek to remind himself of his equality at all times, but especially when he is most happily engrossed in his inequality. He will guard against the temptation to forget that he was a man before he became a philosopher, and that he will perhaps remain a man after philosophy has ceased to have any significance for him. It will be his problem, not chiefly to popularize the expression of his philosophical results, but rather to humanize himself. A philosophy popular in form is not necessarily a human philosophy. It is not ordinarily popular to mean a great deal by what one says, even if the saying is couched in the simplest of terminologies. I have never been able to understand how it can give a thinker satisfaction to see the delicate ramifications of his thought obscured, its meaning distorted, and its profundity trivialized, in order to gain for it a currency of doubtful import. But, on the other hand, if he believes that the essential equality of men is more than an orator's phrase, and that a brotherhood is possible in which this essential equality reveals itself, then he will not be able to find his deepest self or his essential happiness in the realization of purely intellectual values. He will instead seek to permeate his philosophical pursuits with a consciousness that robs his differential perfection of its arrogance, its power to humiliate the excluded. He will strive to incorporate his reflection in a dedication that all can understand; for it is not in talent but in its inward dedication, and it is not in scope and quantity of activity but in its quality and intensity that the human unity may be found which every man is called upon to express.

Here I am confronted with my topic. For if superiority in the scope and accuracy and synoptic unity and perspicuity of his knowledge and reflection is what marks the thinker, and separates him from his fellow men, what can be more obvious than that the consciousness of his limitations and his ignorance is a bond which again unites him with them? Doubtless there are better ways in which one may seek an approach to the democratic idea. But it has seemed to me not inappropriate to the present occasion to explore certain considerations of logic and metaphysics, in order to seek in these disciplines a reflection of its reality. Uncertainty, insecurity, risk, are characters that qualify human existence essentially, and rank as constituting factors in its metaphysical structure — this is the theme that I have taken as my point of departure. The further task that I have set for myself is the description of what seems to me the ground of such uncertainty in the structure of consciousness; and, finally, an estimate of the significance of this fact in shaping the fundamental human attitudes.

I

Wherever there is life, there is uncertainty. Uncertainty confronts those who command all the resources of science, as well as those whose lives are overshadowed by the darkest ignorance. No very searching reflection is needed to reveal this fact. The obvious possibility of death at any moment renders literally everything insecure in its relation to the individual human being. To enforce and illustrate this point I need only remind myself in your presence that it is uncertain whether I shall live to finish the reading of this address. Knowledge mitigates insecurity without abolishing it, and the wisest possible use of the most reliable knowledge conceivable involves the taking of risks. Obvious as this truth is to an objective and detached contemplation, it is often exceedingly difficult to preserve amidst the pressing business of life. Success stills the whisper that would remind us of it. For it is human to forget that our success has an aspect that makes it as fundamentally a gift as an achievement, and that the possibilities which talent, knowledge, will, and industry create do not become actualities as a matter of course, or of sheer necessity.

Existence discloses its precariousness in a twofold manner. It confronts us as we face the future, and propose to utilize knowledge for the realization of some human end. The certainty or uncertainty of the knowledge we use has no essential bearing upon the uncertainty inherent in its application. The principles of logic and the formulas of mathematics are no more capable of guaranteeing infallibility in the application than the hypotheses of the most empirical branch of science. But the body of knowledge is itself also permeated by uncertainty, so that the highest attainable truth is an approximation, whose progressive verifications always remain within the bounds of a continual approach to certain proof.

Knowledge is universal, but its successful application in a particular situation (and all action is particular) depends upon individual conditions necessarily external to knowledge in its aspect of universality. It is self-contradictory to assume a theory that mediates between theory and practice, and there is no knowledge so concrete that it could make the use of knowledge as secure as the knowledge itself is sound. In their relation to life the axioms become hypotheses, and all knowledge becomes a system of possibilities. The greater the scope of a man's knowledge, the greater the number of possibilities among which he may and must make his choice for action. There are multiple hypotheses within the sphere of science, since the facts known at any given time are capable of being explained in different ways. But even if these were all eliminated, the fact that no human consciousness is able exhaustively to penetrate any situation in all its concreteness would necessarily prevent such unified science from becoming univocal in its application. No increase in the precision and scope of our knowledge, no intensification of our powers of reflection can rob the future of its alternative possibilities. Rather does every increase in the effectiveness of our intellectual instrumentalities multiply the confronting alternatives; so that the more one knows, the more difficult it is to reach a conclusion or a decision. Hence it is that when knowledge is not controlled, and reflection is permitted to run wild in its own infinite ramifications, it tends to paralyze action or indefinitely postpone it, instead of affording it guidance; thus it fails of realizing the end that constitutes the ultimate reason for its existence. In this way, among others, we may verify the proverb that increase of knowledge means increase of sorrow. Reflection and cognition may become an armor so heavy that it impedes and endangers the individual, instead of protecting him.

If taken without qualification, the customary characterization of reflection as the problem-solving activity of the human spirit is likely to be misleading. Reflection is no doubt a factor in the solution of such practical and vital problems as confront the individual, but alone and unaided it is quite powerless to solve any human problem, except such as are already solved, in a certain sense, before reflection upon them begins. When we find ourselves assuming that cognition or reflection determines us univocally to a line of action, it is because we fail to bring our chief underlying presuppositions to consciousness. Or we are perhaps dominated by a predilection for some special possibility, hopeful or despairing; and this excludes from our consciousness alternatives equally possible. The depth of prejudice, the sluggishness of imagination, and the limitations of our intellectual horizon are the chief factors that support an undue exaltation of intellect in the economy of life. The uncertainty that confronts ignorance is simple and undisguised, having no wealth of words in which to express itself. The uncertainty that confronts knowledge is none the less real because it is complicated and seductive, capable of taking on the false appearance of certainty, and eloquent in many tongues. From an absolute point of view the relative difference between more or less of knowledge thus becomes nonessential, since it does not alter essentially the basic conditions of life; it is no sufficient ground for either exaltation or depression, for either pride or envy.

An enthusiasm for the enterprise of knowledge is not incompatible with a consciousness of its limitations. To this the Greeks bear witness, and one in particular, whose

matchless energy of reflection began and ended in ignorance. Everyone knows that Socrates identified that wisdom
which is specifically human with a consciousness of one's
own ignorance, and that it was thus he sought to draw the
boundaries between the human and the divine. The uncertainties which remain after knowledge and reflection have
done their best for us are our tutors and disciplinarians.
They drive us back upon ourselves, and are capable of
evoking forces within us more profound in their significance, more characteristic of our personalities and more decisive of their destiny, than any particular degree of adequacy
or inadequacy in our knowledge. Human faith, elicited by
the demands of our existence on many different levels and
in many different forms, has its disappointments and its vagaries, its trials and its discipline. But it is the deepest con-
structive force of human nature, for without faith the
personality cannot express or constitute itself. I believe,
therefore I speak; I believe, therefore I act; and as I believe,
with its consequences in speech and action, so I am.

I have assumed a distinction between the possession of
knowledge and its application, between its existence and its
use. The limitations of my theme do not permit me to
argue the distinction, except to say that the assumption
seems conformable to the language of daily life, and sometimes also to the language of those thinkers who seek to
erase the distinction by defining knowledge as essentially
identical with knowledge-in-use. For they sometimes indulge in polemics against theories of the nature of knowledge which would lead, in their opinion, to its misuse or
disuse. But an instrument that can be misused or disused
necessarily has an existence of its own, distinguishable from
the realization of its ideal function. An ax does not become
nonexistent when it rests from felling trees, nor does a road

cease to be a road when it is perverted to the uses of a high-wayman. The old controversy over the existence of useless knowledge could never be settled, because nobody knows enough to decide whether a given item of apparently useless information may not really be useful; and in any case the question was not really relevant to the point of principle it was intended to decide. But everybody knows that there is such a thing as unused knowledge, and this seems to me decisive of the epistemological issue referred to.

Assuming the validity of this distinction, I proceed to ask whether within the sphere of knowledge itself, as apart from its use, there exists a reflection, a secondary expression, of the fundamental uncertainty of life. Logical and mathematical problems appear to be soluble through the attainment of clarity of thought alone, and it seems as if I do not need to err in these fields provided I thoroughly understand my meanings. My objects have ideal being only, and ideal existence needs no other verification than that which consists in being clearly conceived. But even intellectual clarity is not entirely free from illusion; the troublesome duality between appearance and reality obtains here also, and what seems to be a self-evidencing insight may later reveal itself as a confusion of thought. The absence of a reference to factual existence in its particularity and concreteness absolves such knowledge from one species of verification only, the verification peculiarly characteristic of the natural and the historial sciences. But the need of that species of verification which consists in a possibility of the repetition of the insight, and of its communicability to other minds, still remains. And this species of verification, like the other, is never final; at its best it passes at once into a memory, which, like every other form of memory, stands in need of verification on its own account.

That the concrete sciences do not claim absolute finality for any of their results, it is here needless to elucidate. The historical material upon which such sciences are based, and to which they again refer, is infinite; no observation or reflection can exhaustively penetrate it. Every conclusion results from an arbitrary stoppage of the inquiry, and is therefore as a matter of course subject to revision in the light of fuller knowledge. Every scientific truth is an approximation. The maximum of intellectual insight with respect to any scientific problem is to command the available evidence so as to understand its force; when this has been achieved, the genuine scientist or historian will scarcely feel the need of adding a subjective faith in the results at which he has arrived, a firm conviction that they cannot be overturned. A later age, with more evidence at its command, will possibly draw different conclusions; and, if it is afflicted with as much folly as our own, will doubtless subject our science to ridicule from the lofty standpoint of its own infallibility. In scientific matters, assurances and protestations are the mark of imperfect understanding, and the crown of infallibility is most fitly worn by those who do not at first hand command the evidence that happens to be available, and who have not subjected themselves to the discipline that would enable them to estimate its force.

II

When we seek the ground of this situation in the structure of experience, we are confronted with a radical dualism. Human consciousness is a synthesis of two factors: the ideal and the real,[12] the logical and the existential. The presence of this duality in the form of a synthesis makes certainty and uncertainty possible; their persistent incommensurability makes uncertainty an inescapable actuality.

Time and space are separating principles, introducing fragmentariness and incompleteness into human experience. The idealities of consciousness serve in their own way to complete the incomplete, yielding the possibility of a sort of wholeness to life at each point of time and space; but only in an imperfect and limited manner. This fact remains as a mark of our finitude, and constitutes an effective obstacle to the attainment of that certainty which is tantamount to objective demonstration.

The duality of ideal and real is the logical foundation for both certainty and uncertainty. If consciousness consisted merely of reals, there could be no question of either, seeing that there could in that case be no questions at all. Everything would merely be; but whether precariously or securely is an issue that could not be raised. For all issues are raised in terms of idealities that refer to realities. If consciousness on the other hand were merely a "bloodless ballet of categories," everything again would simply be, though in another sense of the term being. It is the varied forms of cross reference between these two factors, and their distinctness in their synthesis, that gives rise to certainty and uncertainty. The duality of datum and meaning is a form of the duality of ideal and real. This distinction has been referred to the distinction between the certain and the precarious, with the effect of apparently softening or eliminating the dualism. What is taken as certain in any cognitive situation is in this view identified with datum, while what is recognized as precarious is said to constitute meaning. This explanation sets the cart before the horse, explaining meaning in terms that presuppose it, and resolving our dualism at the expense of failing to analyze the concept of the precarious. Certain and precarious alike are matters of meaning, and both involve a relationship between ideality and reality.

What is true of these concepts, the immediate subject of this address, holds true also of a host of related categories. Truth and error, knowledge and its objective reference, language and symbolism, faith and doubt, intent and verification, refer in various ways to this primary distinction between ideal and real as the ground of their possibility. The attempt to elucidate such concepts on the basis of a monistic presupposition, idealistic or realistic, seems bound to fail. Or if it succeeds, it is only by surreptitiously introducing at the rear door some category that has just been ostentatiously dismissed at the front.

The irreducibility of ideal and real may seem to offer a challenge to the reason, just as every dualism appears to certain thinkers a rock of offense and a stone of stumbling. But this happens only when the reason, in its vaulting ambition, undertakes the responsibility for a creation of the world out of its own resources. When the reason thus tries to bring about a synthesis of discrete factors, it abolishes their discreteness, since it is not capable of an actual synthesis, but only of a logical unification. The explanation of particulars in terms of logically prior universals leaves their particularity intact; the explanation of relative dualities in terms of abstract unities does not abolish the dualities taken as a point of departure. Everything found is explained in terms of the found; and thus it is not explanation that is prior to finding, but ultimately finding that is prior to explanation. If therefore an irreducible dualism seems so obtrusively something found that it cries out for an explanation in the form of a reduction, we have first to ask whether an abstract principle of unification really can be found. The imperative impulse to explain away the dualisms of experience, by reducing either one member to the other or both to a third, is a misunderstanding which arises from assuming that explanation creates the found instead of presupposing it. The actual synthesis of discrete factors in existence is *toto caelo* different from their logical unification, and is something the reason need not take upon its conscience, any more than it need assume the task of showing why anything exists, deduce the actual from the possible, or one quality from another.

The current explanations of language, symbols, ideas, and the like often attempt to operate without recognizing any other order of being than the real or existential. The consequence is that a surreptitious or merely instinctive use of categories not avowedly recognized becomes a necessity, in order to preserve for the account a minimum of plausibility. Already the Greeks were compelled to face problems whose solution depended upon a clear recognition of the ideal-real distinction, or upon its prosaic and unsentimental clarification. I say prosaic and unsentimental, for it seems to me that it was the aesthetic or ethicoaesthetic enthusiasm of Plato that seduced him into the mazes of a lyrical mystification of what was otherwise a genuine logical discovery. One may well hold with Plato, and with Socrates before him, that without the recognition of ideal forms the concept of knowledge becomes impossible; and this without either subscribing to Plato's principle that science is only of the unchanging, or sympathizing with his metaphysical hypostatization of the forms. Science and opinion alike involve ideal entities *in* which to think; but it is only when reflection becomes epistemological that we also think *about* them. As instruments of knowledge they need to be capable of recapture in their absolute identity with themselves, under whatever change of circumstance in the knower or his object, if only in order that such change of circumstance may be subject to recognition. In so far they may be said to escape the temporal mutability that attaches to the real objects whose knowledge they mediate. One may also hold with Plato that false statements are reduced to meaningless sounds, and hence lose even their falsity, unless their meanings are constituted in a kind of existence that is also nonexistence. This view is one that Plato supports by a doctrine of the mingling of the categories, in which existence and nonexistence are denied the status of true contradictories. One may find it necessary to clarify this dictum by adding, what Plato was loath to concede, that it is precisely the being of his ideal forms that so merges with nonbeing that it becomes representative of nonexistence. This kind of being is a necessary condition for fitness to serve as the logical content of predication whether true or false, whether referring to the changing or to the permanent.

In modern philosophy the concept of the *idea* has been emasculated beyond the possibility of any use for knowledge, by its reduction to the status of a psychical real. When so regarded, it becomes an object of which one may presumably become aware, but it is no longer an instrument for the apprehension of other objects. Knowledge then becomes awareness of ideas, not an apprehension of things. An idea is a synthesis of psychical reality and logical ideality. Its ideal and intentional character gives it its revealing function. Take this aspect away and thoughts become blind and windowless, obtruding their own immediate existence between ourselves and the world. In so far it is not surprising that many modern thinkers have adopted the desperate expedient of rejecting ideas altogether, though it seems to me more hopeful to revise our conceptions of them.

Language is in a similar situation. Extraordinary efforts have been expended upon the project of explaining language as some sort of a real relation between reals, a conjunction between words and things. The watchword of this theory is: *vox et res, et praeterea nihil*. It is assumed that the meaning of words is a matter of context, or of leading within a context. But context in any sense germane to this purpose is a consequence of the ideal intent attached to words, and hence presupposes what it is assumed to explain. In a purely realistic sense of the words " context," or " leading," they do nothing to explain meaning; since an infinite mass of irrelevant material is included within the " real" context, and the causal leading includes the logically relevant only by exception. Hobbes, in spite of his nominalistic terminology, had a much too adequate grasp of the nature of the logical to identify it with a real aspect of something real. In expounding the relation between the premises of a syllogism and its conclusion, he insists that the former are not the cause of the latter, since " speech is not the cause of speech." In other words, implication is not an existential relation, as is causation, but a logical one. Speech taken as voice, or as bodily reaction, certainly is the cause of speech; but taken as the ideal content of which its existential aspect is the vehicle, it is neither cause nor effect. It is not by any real character peculiar to sounds that thought is to be explained; on the contrary, it is thought and its ideality that explain the word-character of words. Symbols have of course an immediate existence of their own. But it is not their immediate character that makes them symbols, but the fact that they mediate an ideal content, yielding an intent which directs itself upon an external existent, other than that of the symbol's own immediacy. Symbols do not explain thought; it is thought that explains symbols.

Truth is not a real relation between reals. A correspondence between reals (and it makes no difference that one of them may be regarded as a psychical entity) is merely resemblance, and resemblance and truth are not identical concepts. Just as what is true of one Lincoln penny is not true of another, so one real in general cannot be true of another, or have it for its object. Logical coherence within an inclusive system of meanings is inadequate to posit the concept of truth. If such meanings are understood to involve a reference beyond themselves, a more fundamental form of verification is presupposed than that which is given in logical coherence. Truth is the fulfillment, actual or possible, of logical intent; error is nonfulfillment. But fulfillment is a relation between ideality and reality; it has no meaning in the relation between idealities or realities by themselves.

The fundamental contrast thus variously exhibited is *sui generis*. An attempt to find a parallel in the heterogeneity of two dissimilar reals would be futile and misleading. For ideal and real do not differ in essence, but in existence. The difference is exemplified in the relation between promise and performance, a plan and its realization, a possibility and its corresponding actuality. Ideality is intent; reality is fulfillment of intent.

A consciousness in which idealities function is a mediating consciousness. But since ideal and real do not as such differ in essence, it becomes misleading to think of mediation as a process of transforming one real into another. Cognition as a mediatory function is therefore not the discovery or creation of a peculiar class of cognitive objects, having special characters making them peculiarly effective as instruments. The recognition of a certain experience as noncognitive is itself a cognitive function, an act of classification. But if classification is the discovery of cognitive objects, we should have to suppose the miracle of a noncognitive experience, in the very act of being recognized as such, thereby becoming a cognitive experience. Knowledge becomes a blind instrument of unconscious forces, if the ideal content of a mediating function is different in essence from the real which it mediates. Such a theory of knowledge instinctively posits as its own medium a different sort of knowledge from that of which it gives an account, a knowledge that sees the difference in essence, and hence transcends the blindness of the knowledge with which it deals.

The mediate is the immediate. The character and qualities of existents are not external to thought; it is only their existence that constitutes for thought an unassimilable thing-in-itself. Existence refuses to become incorporated in thought; it is the only one of all the categories that is not given when it is truly conceived. For the thought of an actuality is not itself that actuality, but the corresponding possibility.

If ideal and real were not homogeneous in essence, knowledge could not be of *what* a thing *is;* if they were not heterogeneous in existence, knowing a thing and being that thing would be the same. But since there is a difference between knowing and being, knowledge stands in need of verification. Verification is the process in which the claim of knowledge is made good. It consists of a confrontation of an ideality and its own intended real within the unity of a single experience. The correspondence experienced in verification receives its cognitive significance not as resemblance, but through the intent which is the essence of a functioning ideality, its power of reference and consequent identification.

In a finite experience idealities and realities are given only fragmentarily and in succession. Presented reals may be felt without being known, the corresponding idealities being absent; logical contents may be had which transcend the boundaries set by the presented existents. Memory, expectation, and general knowledge involve logical idealities which serve in some degree to bridge the gaps in the presentation of the existential, thus making possible a relative control of the momentary impression and impulse.

It has sometimes been denied that existence is ever given, thus making it exclusively an object of intent and belief. If this were the case, the concept of verification would have to be rejected as an illusion. Knowledge would be a claim destined never to enjoy the satisfaction of even a partial validation. It would be a seeking that knows no finding, a question without an answer. The partial and relative discrepancy upon which we have insisted would in this view become complete and absolute; the origin of the very idea of certainty, and therefore also of uncertainty, would become incomprehensible. Experience would in no way be distinguishable from imagination, and all experiment would be pure speculation. One cannot legitimately escape this dilemma by limiting the theory to the terms of the external world, withdrawing its scheme of relations from the scope of the theory's skepticism. The dialectic that applies to the terms applies with equal force to the relations. If existences are unknown as to their terms, then they are also unknown as to the relations that the terms sustain. Nor can it be known whether the data which we take to represent them are mere symbols or not. An absolute likeness is precisely as probable as an absolute unlikeness; the only utterance with respect to them that is free from self-contradiction is the negative utterance of a confession of ignorance. It is only with respect to objects whose real nature is known that I am able to recognize certain representations as merely symbolic. The skepticism here alluded to is logically possible, but practically unmotivated. The arguments by which it seeks to give itself a positive status are necessarily self-contradictory, assuming a knowledge in the premises that the conclusion takes occasion to deny.

It is difficult to doubt that the terms of my own existence are presented. My own existence is surely something more than the conclusion of a syllogism, even if it remains true that its entire external, empirical content is never at any time completely given. As for other things and persons, there is a complication involved which offers a difficulty. In the first place it must be remembered that the sensible appearances that we accept as testimony for the existence of external things are themselves reals, and not mere logical essences. All perception involves a presupposition, a presupposition that constitutes its heart and soul as an intentional act. Perception is the interpretation of its constituent sensory data as self-presentations of the perceived object. This interpretation is in its detail subject to an immanent correction; but it is not subject to cancellation except at the cost of wiping out the function of perception altogether. Within this presupposition sense data serve as partial verifications of our ideas of external things. They are thus a synthesis of two discrete categories, being both *effects* and *appearances* in one. If they are regarded merely as effects, perception is robbed of its cognitive and revelatory character, at least in its primary relation to things; the cognitive function is pushed one step farther back, the sense data themselves becoming primary objects of cognition. To regard the sensible appearances solely as revelations is to ignore the natural matrix of interaction in which knowledge has its birth and by which it is conditioned. With respect to the terms of my own existence, then, verification is directly possible; since knowledge and being are here capable of being united in a conscious synthesis. With respect to other existences, verification has meaning within the presupposition which constitutes the essence of perception, albeit it suffers here from a certain indirection. But this indirection must not be identified with the remoteness from existence of conceptual thought, unless we wish wholly to reject the testimony of perception with respect to itself, and confound the ideality of thought with the reality of sense.

It remains, however, a significant fact that no concrete object is ever so completely given existentially, whether directly or under the perceptual presupposition just referred to, that its idea can be said to have obtained complete verification. Time and space, as they separate promise from performance, and all plans from their realization, so also do they separate the claims of knowledge from their complete validation. There is thus an inevitable incommensurability between the scope and extent of the ideal and the scope and extent of the real as given in experience, which makes cognition in its perfection a desideratum, both in its direction toward the ideal and in its direction toward the real. The incommensurability lends to the ideal its practical function, and yet at the same time prevents it from exercising that function without risk. An experience in which an exhaustive description of all things was confronted with an equally exhaustive presentation of the same as its verification would also be an experience in which nothing could happen, and so nothing would remain to be done. Thus we seem to be faced with the paradox that it is the logical imperfection of knowledge that makes possible its practical perfection. If there is no certainty without immediate verification, and if verification means the cessation of practice with respect to what it verifies, it follows that to concede a practical function to knowledge is *ipso facto* to admit the insecurity of its exercise.

III

If this analysis of the structure of experience is well founded, it follows that human life cannot move forward without the constant and repeated rendering of the subjective decision which we call belief. Belief incorporates knowledge, in that it is a choice among the alternatives that knowledge presents, but it does not rest upon knowledge; for its decision is not commensurable with an objective certitude. Belief has varied forms and objects. It ranges from the trivial to the sublime; it may be the childish confidence of a naïve immediacy, or it may be that faith which is born in the crisis of a profound breach with such immediacy. But in all its forms it is a subjective commitment to an objective uncertainty, and concerns the question of existence or nonexistence. The understanding formulates the *what;* belief comes to rest in the *that.* The completeness of its subjective commitment may vary. Its movement may be merely tentative and experimental; or it may constitute itself as a definitive summing up of the total meaning of that life with which, as a whole, the individual is forbidden to experiment, if for no other reason than that he has but one life to live. But whether it is tentative or decisive, belief is never the immediate and necessary consequence of a purely objective motivation. The universal presence of objective uncertainty implies the universal presence of a subjective motivation in the faiths of men, however much they may conceal it from themselves by allowing habit to dull their sensibilities, or by following thoughtlessly in the footprints of others, or by indulging themselves in an overconfidence in their own cleverness and insight.

If none of the more transient and trivial responses to the call of existence can be made without risk, as is indeed generally admitted, it is surely thoughtless to imagine or demand that the fundamental response which we call a view of life, and upon which the others rest, should be found by way of objective certainty. A view of life — that single decisive choice of attitude, which, without losing its identity with itself, can become commensurable with every finite situation, declinable in all the innumerable cases that the grammar of existence affords — how should such a view be found if he who seeks it seeks it only on condition that he be made demonstrably safe from the risk of error, demanding here a fullness of objective guaranty that is denied him in every minor relation of life? No, indeed; the basic decision of life is so far from being made for us that it is our deepest subjective responsibility. It is so far from being the most adequately supported by a preponderance of the evidence that may be gleaned by a maximum of knowledge that it is precisely here that the relative advantage of superior learning is most completely neutralized. In relation to the substance of life, the aristocratic privileges enjoyed by superior intelligence when dealing with its accidents are negatived, and the basic democracy of human existence unmistakably asserted.

Uncertainty is the stimulus of interest. If every choice could be objectively determined, it would be reduced to a matter of course, an automatic process lacking in the subjective tension which is the form of appropriation for all genuine happiness. Intensity of pathos is the measure of our capacity for profound joy. Uncertainty throws the in-

dividual back upon himself, unlocks the hidden energies
of his spirit, and affords him the opportunity to form those
ideal resolutions of the will in which the life of the spirit
is realized. Strife and struggle, anxiety and hope, fear and
trembling, despair and faith, are the disciplinarians that
fashion the personality. The lofty calm in which a disinterested, or merely aesthetically interested, contemplation of
idealities is indulged has been called the life of pure spirit,
in contrast with a life dominated by the natural urgings
of the human animal. This spirit lives by a retreat from
life, and is an expression of aristocratic privilege. The passionate faith in an existence that commands the total interest and concrete pathos of the individual is the distinctively human spirit in its highest expression. It lives by
pressing forward, and is not a privilege of the few. It is
a fundamental human passion; and the passions, as Lessing
says, place all men on a footing of equality: "*Die Leiden-
schaften machen Menschen allen gleich.*"

But is not probability [18] the guide of life, and is it not subject to an objective calculation? The calculus of probability
is a very remarkable invention of the human mind, seemingly capable of distilling knowledge from ignorance and
truth from error, transforming admitted uncertainties into
demonstrated truths. Where certainty is unattainable, there
is at least evidence; and it rarely or never happens that the
weight of evidence is equally balanced. The predicament
of Burdian's ass seems quite fictitious, one not likely to offer
itself in the infinite complex called human life. I have only
to seek and follow the preponderance of evidence, in order
that my every problem may receive an objective solution.
While knowledge would not in that case abolish uncertainty, it would indeed univocally determine choice. The
main movement of life would thus be directed outwardly,

toward a greater and greater objectivity. The subjective would be reduced to a troublesome or negligible appendage, to be eliminated as far as is humanly possible. Even latitudinarians in ethics have on this point sometimes displayed a most exacting rigorism; for some of them have made it an absolute moral duty never to believe anything except that which is supported by a preponderance of evidence.

I must confess that I find in myself no echo of this moral principle, nor can I subscribe to Bishop Butler's maxim in all its universality. The assertion of the moral principle seems to me to rest upon a confusion of things very different. It seeks to enforce intellectual honesty. But it errs in assuming that belief is or should be a simple function of the intellect alone. Let us have intellectual honesty by all means; the preponderance of evidence is what it is, and should of course be acknowledged for what it is. The probable is the probable, and the improbable is the improbable. It sometimes happens that men attempt to carry water on both shoulders. They desire, for example, to enjoy the advantage of the moral elasticity that comes from being in the minority. But they are not willing to pay the price, for they also want to enjoy the peace and security and objectivity that come from being in the majority, and so we find them speaking and writing in the name of the many, but against a supposed majority. And so also in this connection: men wish for one reason or another to believe in the improbable, but they also wish to claim for themselves a higher knowledge, a knowledge in advance of the age, in virtue of which the belief in question is no longer improbable, but even certain. Such double-mindedness betrays a sorry confusion of mind, and is ultimately rooted in cowardice.

There are indeed situations in which there exists no ethically defensible motive for believing contrary to the calculations of the understanding. But there are also situations in which the refusal to venture on the basis of an improbability betrays sluggishness of spirit. I need not remind my hearers that I am speaking of belief as a factor in the forward movement of the personal life, and not of that attenuated function which we sometimes call belief, but which is simply and solely the casting up of intellectual accounts. The conviction that is sometimes attached to scientific conclusions is really a work of supererogation; what the intellect requires is nothing more than insight into the available evidence and its probative force. Such insight is a purely objective function; it lacks the subjectivity characteristic of belief, and the retention of the name in this connection makes it necessary to distinguish between objective and subjective belief. From the standpoint of life, the former is otiose; the latter alone is a vital and moving force.

In a concrete situation, where action is the outcome of belief, it may and does happen that both the claims and the responsibilities of the personality burst the bonds of a calculation of probabilities. The actual is not identical with the possible, nor the possible with the probable. The probable and the possible are categories that, while objective in their reference, have their grounds in subjective limitations. Probability is not an objective force in events, working to bring them about in proportion to its preponderance. And the same holds true of the possible. The seemingly impossible happens, and the event that has the odds overwhelmingly against it does come to pass. The realm of the possible is an untamed giant, and it is a stupid delusion to imagine that this giant has been tamed and imprisoned in a flimsy network of prudent calculations. Life teaches that noble enthusiasms are seldom born out of the calculations of the understanding. Those who must have a reasonable assurance of success before venturing on any project rarely venture anything worth-while. But the noble spirits who have chosen causes that needed to be served, instead of causes whose chances of success were such as made them seem capable of serving their representatives, have usually had the probabilities against them when they ventured. Should their enthusiasm have blinded them to this fact, there are doubtless contemporary critics to remind them, and to remind them also of their folly. And if their efforts finally meet with success, other critics of the same order will imagine that they understand the necessity of that success, finding in the category of cause and effect an excuse for interpreting the transition immanently, as the necessary unfolding of what was originally present. This latter wisdom seems to me the greater folly. For it was doubtless quite true that it was improbable. But it is nonsense to interpret any change as necessary,[14] since necessity is a category that expresses self-identity, its principle being that a thing is what it is.

Belief in the improbable is not self-contradictory; neither is it inherently unethical. To retain confidence in another's integrity even when appearances are against him, and while the understanding is still unable to exhibit them as mere appearances, is surely not unethical; it is rather evidence of a genuine goodness on the part of the believer. The maxim of probability as highest principle is the wisdom of those who have forgotten what enthusiasm is, and that it is man's chief crown of glory. It is a principle that would abolish altogether the sense of wonder. Wonder is a passion which has its childish vagaries, its disappointments, and its death in despair; but it has also its rebirth to a new life, and is the beginning and the end of a more profound apprehension of reality.

The more trivial the issues that confront me, the more

mediocre the ends I set myself, the more commensurate
will my decision be with a calculation of probabilities. The
more ideally significant the issues, the more deeply my decision works back to qualify and transform my life, the less
will it be possible to make them commensurate with such
considerations. There comes a point in the scale of human
decisions when these cease chiefly to be an expression of
outward circumstance, and of the knowledge of circumstance, and become instead an expression of the quality of
the personality that decides. We begin life by submitting
reality to a cross-examination, exploring its secrets for what
we imagine is our advantage. But at a critical juncture the
tables are turned, and reality becomes a cross-examiner,
compelling us to answer so as to reveal what there exists or
comes to birth within us. It is then that the spirit becomes
mature, and its answers yield the fundamental faiths upon
which our lives are borne forward. The relation between
objective and subjective in reference to belief is this, that
the more fundamental the faith, the less does a difference
between more or less of knowledge and of objective reflection play a decisive role in its adoption.

This can be elucidated by reference to an example or two.
There is an aristocratic disease that attacks chiefly those
whose situation in life is such as to permit them the luxury
of diverting the energies of thought from its primary task
of thinking other things to the task of thinking itself, in
an effort to construe its own validity. This effort inevitably
gives rise to a fundamental skepticism. How can the intellect make good its claim to think the past and the future,
when every thought is limited in its existence to the present? How can one thing possibly know another thing?
How can numerically distinct thoughts, having different
psychological and physical contexts, identify the same topic

of discourse and carry the same meaning? When such doubts arise, it is evident that no calculation of probabilities will suffice to silence them. Once having taken command of the course of thought, they can effectively sustain themselves indefinitely, interpreting in their own spirit every opposite consideration. The cure for such doubts does not lie in more reflection, but in a new point of departure for reflection. Such a point of departure is related to the preceding doubt as an act of faith which constitutes a genuine leap. Its motivation is and can be nothing but the felt presence of an elementary human need, namely, the need of finding in thought a guide and an inspiration of action, rather than the blank futility of a paralysis of all action. The plain man believes in the validity of thought instinctively. The logician is no nearer than he to a demonstration that it really is valid; he is in precisely the same situation of having to believe or perish, and his only advantage is that he may gain a more acute consciousness of his necessity through being afflicted with the disease of doubt.

The inductive leap is an example of the same necessity. Is the correction of our errors and the revision of our formulas in an effort more closely to approximate the ultimate structure of events a futile occupation, like the gambler's everlasting search for an infallible system? Does reality perhaps have no structure, the appearance of law in things being merely the accidental result of humanly superficial observation and humanly limited experience? Or is our progress real because its goal is real? Is it a search that has meaning and an approximation that actually brings us nearer? This doubt cannot be quieted deductively, since it does not deal with the implications of ideas, but with a question of existence. It cannot be disproved inductively, since it attacks the very principle by which particular facts can be regarded as evidence for anything beyond themselves. It is a faith rooted in human need; the scientist and the philosopher have no other recourse with respect to it than to yield to the universal human impulse. What is the upshot of Kant's deduction of the categories but a demonstration that without them no experience can be orderly? And is not this at bottom an appeal to human need, the need of food and shelter, and the need of a conscious command of the resources of existence relative to the provision of elementary necessities?

How strange that the highest principles of the reason should appear to be beggarly articles of faith! And yet this would seem to be inevitable if reason is to retain a foothold in existence, not avoiding its responsibilities by emigrating to a new continent, where existence and nonexistence do not matter.

I pass to an ethical example. Is the sense of obligation a genuine revelation of my situation, or merely a passing illusion? There are men bold enough to deny that they have this consciousness; and every man doubtless has moments in which the possibility of casting off the yoke of ought appeals to him as an agency of liberation. It has been explained as an anachronism, a survival from a despotic organization of society, living a ghostly existence in the minds of men after its material incarnation has ceased. In the face of such doubts, where is the indisputable evidence for its validity? The exhibition of a more or less precarious finite teleology for the moral consciousness is a misunderstanding of its essence, since such a teleology is incommensurable with its demands. The ethical consciousness is subjectively motivated in moral passion, in an enthusiasm that posits the true being of man in a relation to something higher than himself, justifying his exercise of a mastery over nature only in and through the fact that he has himself become a servant. Moral science neither creates nor validates this enthusiasm, but rests upon this consciousness as its underlying presupposition. Where moral passion is lacking, objective reflection cannot produce it. The need for an ethical interpretation of life is not indeed the need for food and shelter; but shall we therefore say that it is less fundamental to human nature? And is this need not found in an intensity approximating ideal proportions, as often in the ignorant as in the wise, in a cobbler as often as in a professor of philosophy? Without denying the significance of ethical science, it should be clear that the basic attitude of spirit is the essential element of the moral consciousness. And this is not a matter of knowledge, but of depth and specific quality of pathos.

As one who confesses to the need of religious categories for his own life and its interpretation, may I select for my final illustration the so-called problem of the existence of God. Every man feels, at least transiently, a need to find an explanation of his existence and its conditions in terms of a cause that can accept responsibility, and can discharge this responsibility by assigning to his life a goal capable of enlisting his wholehearted interest and devotion. In this sense to ask concerning the whence and the whither of life is not to ask a scientific question, nor one that can be answered by an appeal to learning of any kind, philosophical or theological or scientific. The problem is human, not scholastic. The structural elements of the world are indeed called causes, but they are not such as are capable of accepting responsibility, not even for their own existence or behavior. The laws of nature give no direction toward a goal, being themselves necessarily neutral toward all goals in order to serve all, and therefore neutral as between good and evil. The entire system of scientific explanations, construed in terms of their present status or in terms of their ideal perfection, seems incapable of satisfying the deepest human demand for explanation. The most profound explanation is the discovery of a teleology that satisfies the deepest need; that which is good in itself needs no explanation, but is itself the explanation of other things.

The religious evaluation of the need of God [15] is that it constitutes man's highest perfection. It is not a need specifically germane to the business of the scientist; it is a need that characterizes man as man, and in this supreme passion all men are made truly equal. The attempt to satisfy it by scientific researches or by dialectical developments is a misunderstanding which reduces it to a relativity. The proofs for the existence of God are merely more or less adequate formulations of the question. The search among the external values of existence (orderliness of plan, ingenuity of contrivance, beauty of appearance) for a perfection in the works of God that should adequately verify his own perfection is a search that ends in indecision as it begins in doubt. It suffers from an unconscious self-contradiction, since it seeks to establish in the world as conceived without God a perfection of teleology that would make him superfluous if it could be found. It is not the perfection, but the imperfection of the world, that stirs the mind to a search for communion with the divine. God is the answer to the capacity in man for an infinite interest. The faith that is born of this need and interest can maintain itself only by a constant renewal of its victory over objective uncertainty and subjective despair. It is always in deep waters, always struggling for existence against objections and difficulties; and yet it is the only form in which man can find God. The religious life has of course, like every other life, its immediacies and its confirmations; but, as lived in time, it cannot escape the possibility of an ambiguous interpretation of its experiences. Its decision is therefore not a possession, but a renewal; it is not safely guaranteed by any sort of objective authority, but subjectively earned again and again. It is not an inert complacency, but a victory over uncertainties and improbabilities and impossibilities.

I have not proposed to offer a criticism of human beliefs. Such criticism is certainly a desideratum, since human faiths are of varying content and value. The content of belief may be noble, sublime, ridiculous, or abhorrent; its form may be a childlike naïveté, or a mature breach with all naïve and immediate valuations. What I have tried to set forth are certain preliminary considerations: that there is a subjective factor in all beliefs, corresponding to the objective uncertainty which they resolve; that the human attitudes that constitute the substance of life are faiths that cling to that which is not completely known, not logical insights into demonstrated verities; that these faiths are presuppositions for reflection and not the necessary outcome of reflection, retaining the status of being presuppositions even after reflection upon them. Reflection is a broker which mediates between the particulars of a given or posited transcendence. The transcendence itself is either given, or posited by passion, and here reflection can only recognize its own impotence to add a cubit to a man's stature.

A criticism of fundamental beliefs is therefore a criticism of passions, not of knowledge. A lower and imperfect passion can be corrected and transcended only by a higher and more disciplined passion. Passion rather than knowledge is the more adequate and concrete expression of the existential situation, since it is the mark of transition, and human existence is essentially in transition. Either passionless contemplation is itself the expression of a negative passion rejecting the forward movement of life or it is an irrelevance to a criticism of beliefs. The important considerations with respect to any confession of faith, says Nietzsche, are: What sort of heaven does it picture? and, With what courage does it inspire the believer? This posits the subjective principle I have here been urging. Hostile as Nietzsche is to that interpretation of life which I would avow, his pathos evidently having been profoundly offended, nay, wounded by the religious consciousness, it seems to me possible to learn from this author more on this point than from most modern writers; for he grasps the issues essentially, knows that they concern the health or disease of the soul, and fights his battles on relevant ground. It has been said that only two sorts of men really know anything about love: the happy and the unhappy lovers; mere spectators remain outsiders. And so with every other fundamental passion, including religion. The criticism of belief is a field only for those thinkers who know how to invest themselves from head to foot in the universal garment of humanity, the pathos of a concrete personality facing the concrete uncertainties of existence. This pathos is essentially the same for the wise and the unwise, the scholar and the plain man; in the realization of this fact we become conscious of the essential democracy of life.

VI

Supernaturalism — Source of Moral Power

From Professor Swenson's Introduction to The Religious
Thought of Søren Kierkegaard, *by Eduard Geismar. Augs-
burg Publishing House, 1937.*

SØREN KIERKEGAARD was a many-sided entity, not to be
exhausted in a phrase or understood from a single point
of view. Nevertheless, I wish here to try to emphasize an
essential and characteristic trait of his spirit — namely, his
unique power of bringing home a moral challenge to the
minds of his readers.

The capacity to preach without descending to trivialities,
and without ever striking a note of false pathos, is a very
rare thing — perhaps the rarest of all accomplishments —
especially among the "scientific" theologians. Of the early
thinkers in the Christian community perhaps Tertullian
and Saint Augustine were among those most mighty in
moral pathos; in later times Pascal, Luther, the William
Law of *A Serious Call to a Devout and Holy Life,* John
Bunyan, and several among the mystics. In the English
and American literature of the nineteenth century, Ruskin
and Emerson and Carlyle were lay preachers of power. Yet
in my opinion Kierkegaard easily surpasses all the great
names on this list, which is not exhaustive but illustrative,
in his sensitiveness to the ideal in all spheres of life, in his
power of persuasive delineation, in the firmness of his grip

upon essentials, in conceptual clarity and precision, and in reflective sophistication. His aesthetic pathos covers the entire range of a gifted poet's fundamental moods; he produces pure poetic effects in prose. His moral pathos is a raging conflagration which will not be extinguished. It is safeguarded from sentimentalism on the one hand and priggishness on the other by an omnipresent and equally proportioned sense of humor that never lets him forget his own personal relativity. A profound pathos appears also in the works of Friedrich Nietzsche, and on this pathos is based his vivid and spontaneous energy of evaluation. But Nietzsche is lacking in an adequately proportioned sense of humor. The quality of pathos is something in which recent thinkers seem to be woefully lacking. Some find Bertrand Russell's *A Free Man's Worship* strong in pathos; I find it empty and strutting rhetoric. In reading many a contemporary talent's finely spun web of reflection, one is sometimes tempted to wonder whether the man has ever lived as a human being. For a wholehearted commitment to the essential tasks of life gives pathos, and also gives a sense of humor. An intense life lived in reflective terms cannot fail to discover contradictions everywhere, and such value contradictions are the stuff out of which the comic is made.

What are the sources in Kierkegaard of the extraordinary moral power that even the casual reader comes soon to feel? It seems to me that his personality has three springs of such power: the disinterestedness that marks his authorship; his flaming sincerity; and his aggressive and powerful and full-blooded supernaturalism. Here I shall emphasize the last, in view of the bad name given to supernaturalism by modern thinkers.

What is supernaturalism in religion, and how can it be said to be a source of moral power? Supernaturalism is

that affirmation of the eternal, and of the necessity of a concretely real relationship to the eternal, without which all
human life tends to become confused and distorted, sinking
into triviality and pointlessness, as being defrauded of its
highest potentiality. It is the affirmation that life is a gift
as well as a task; it is the recognition that each developing
phase of that gift is the starting point for a task, and that
each essential task involves the consciousness of a gift as its
impetus and condition. Such a religiosity is a concrete synthesis of receptivity and activity, expressed in terms of the
human life of a self that knows itself as derivative, not
original or self-posited. That religion with its cognate God-
idea involves such a fundamental receptivity finds well-nigh
universal support in the instinctive consciousness of mankind. It is testified to by John Dewey, aggressive opponent
of supernaturalism in the fundamental principle of his entire view of life, who nevertheless says that the concept of
God is needed in a naturalistic type of religiosity for the
purpose of a recognition of the fact that moral ideas are
not rootless, since "there are forces in nature and society
that generate and support the ideals" [*A Common Faith,*
pp. 51 ff.]. But supernatural religion gives a more concrete
and more decisive expression to this principle. In consequence it stresses gratitude as an underlying and essential
human passion, whose emasculation through the deperson-
alization of the God-idea, and substitution for it of the
abstract fiction of "society" or "humanity," constitutes no
advance, as the philosophers believe, but a retrogression, an
inhumanism robbing life of essential value content, and taking away from every ideal striving its highest and most
powerful inspiration. The religiosity of supernaturalism cultivates thankfulness as a virtue; moreover, it has learned
from human love, which outside of religion is man's highest

ruling and sustaining passion, that "the gift without the giver is bare."

The God-idea of this religiosity is personal as a matter of course; no other type of concept could possibly meet its needs or correspond to its nature. The personality category not only exhibits the highest type of value that experience affords; the person ethically determined is in the last analysis the only abiding value. Such religiosity neither finds nor seeks a basis for its concept of God in the abstractions of mathematical physics, nor in the real or fancied differences between mechanistic and organic principles of organization among the objects of natural science, nor in any of the other pseudo profundities of a modern philosophy of religion; it seeks and finds a basis for the God-idea in the depths of the human heart, and in the ideal for a human life. It originates and culminates in an idealizing personal relationship; its faith is a concrete personal attitude, having for its object a concrete personal attitude. God is thus a person; his will is the everlasting distinction between righteousness and unrighteousness, good and evil; it is goodness and love. Love and righteousness do not attach to impersonal things or essences; the idea of the good is not good. Anything less than a personal life attitude is for a human being something abstract; religion is concrete, expressing in the most concrete manner possible man's personal situation in existence. Such religiosity as we have here outlined understands Aristotle's dictum that man is a social animal in a sense far more profound than Aristotle dreamed, for it includes among the needs of man as social the need of an ideal socius as regulative principle and source of culminating satisfaction. Or, rather, it recognizes that the ideal socius is already there, pressing for a free and unforced admission — for love is not love without a free choice and an unforced devotion — to a companionship by which the eternal life can begin to become the life that pulsates in every fiber of man's being, giving him a happiness that is happiness indeed.

When the eternal, and the life of the eternal, is brought so close to the individual man and pressed so vigorously upon his consciousness as is characteristic of the type of religiosity that Kierkegaard represents, it is impossible to escape a deepening sense of one's own imperfection. And this sense of moral imperfection [16] gives a new and intimate and more significant direction to the moral task, for it determines that task as the reconstruction of the individual and his mode of life. This leads in turn to a more profound receptivity, to a deeper sense of the mode of man's continuing dependence upon the divine. Receptivity and imperfection are thus revealed as cognate categories: each stands for a consciousness that brings about an increased sense of significance for the other. And both together profoundly affect and modify that active expression which in the religious consciousness represents the ethical. Religion stripped of the ethical becomes poetry or metaphysics; religion stripped of receptivity and the sense of imperfection is externalism, and tends to become the thin beer of politics. But the deeper the sense of imperfection, the more passionately profound is the gratitude, and the more powerful is prompting to an ethical striving.

A naturalistic religiosity either thoughtlessly ignores the moral imperfection of the individual, his misuse of freedom, or cultivates a frivolous consciousness of its significance. Who could recount all the miserable subterfuges, the cowardly evasions, the vain and paltry excuses, which in modern literature and thought have been manufactured in order to help the individual evade or escape the sense of guilt?

By a curious inversion the problem has been put as the problem of reconciling the goodness of God with the evil in the world, pretending to succeed or assuming to fail in justifying "the ways of God to men." This is really but a veiled attempt to shift the burden of guilt from man's shoulders to God's, and to make of the individual a fictitious third party, setting himself up to judge in the case between God and other men, a proceeding as morally fatuous as it is dialectically impossible.

I remember once to have remarked in conversation with a colleague that there were two kinds of religion: one for good men and one for bad ones; and that I needed the latter kind. The reply was somewhat to this effect: "But, Swenson, you will never bring the American people to a consciousness of sin." Far be it from me to have the slightest notion, or the faintest intimation of a notion in the farthermost recesses of my most secret mind, that I have any mission or responsibility in this direction. If this is to be done, the ground will first have to be prepared by abandoning completely this abstract and impersonal notion of being a part of the American people, and substituting therefor an individual consciousness. But even if every other American were an angel, and his conscience pure as driven snow, or if not every American, then at least every American professor of philosophy except myself, it would still hold true of me that I stand in need of a religion of pardon and grace, of a religion that offers and effects a relationship to a divine reality that can reconstitute the integrity of the personality. As a child I was told that I needed such a religion, but I did not at first understand this to be so; later I came to understand it. And now at the age of sixty, having spent a lifetime in the use of such powers of reflection as I have, and in the exploration of myself through experience, through the nature of my occupation fortunately free from any finite bonds tying me to an institutional loyalty or to a dogmatic adherence, I still know no better than that what my mother told me was and is the simple truth. But one thing is certain: no man who approaches the God-idea from any other standpoint than from the standpoint of his own moral imperfection will ever have occasion to know the height and breadth and depth of the love of God, which passes all human understanding.

And let it not be forgotten in this connection that the experience just referred to posits a new standard and measure for human reconciliation *inter se,* since the consciousness of the divine creative forgiveness [17] is lost to us when we refuse to forgive our enemies or those who have done us an injury. Here again we see how a deepened receptivity conditions a deepened activity, a more profound consciousness of the moral task and ideal, thus laying deeper foundations for the social life. This is something that Royce has completely forgotten, when he permits his hypothetical traitor theatrically to boast that he will allow none of the gods or men to forgive him (*The Problem of Christianity,* I, p. 266) — an unethical transcription in value terms of the abstract-logical principle of the irrevocableness of the past. When we do not fantastically and absent-mindedly put the traitor in a class all by himself, outside the human race, but quite simply identify him with man as man, confessing our own essential humanity in terms of moral imperfection, we shall have occasion to note how irreligious is the misconstruction, not only of Christianity but of all essential religiosity, that Royce permits himself in order to find an imaginary support in religion for his own metaphysical system.

Because it makes eternity essential, supernatural religion

also makes a distinction between *here* and *there*,[18] between the present life and future life, and thus has an "otherworldly" character. There is scarcely any subject connected with religion on which more nonsense has been written, and will doubtless continue to be written. Suppose we briefly ask what it is that supernatural religion regards as "here" and what as "there." Here is the struggle and the strife, the hardship and the suffering, the discipline and the many errors, together with the "correction" which for the present "seemeth . . . not joyous but grievous," but afterward bears fruit in righteousness. Here is the uncertainty and the risk of failure, the need for faith, for patience, and for courage to make shift with a partial vision, since here "we see in a mirror, darkly." There is the rest and the peace, the final consummation, the consciousness of a victory not again to be jeopardized, the happiness of looking back upon sufferings endured in a good cause. Here is the inevitable sense of moral heterogeneity, enforced upon the consciousness by the struggle with ourselves and with the spirit dominant in the world; there is the sense of belonging, of the traveler arrived at home. A summer excursion upon the calm waters of a sheltered bay induces no longing to reach the shore; but sailors battling in an angry sea and straining every nerve to reach haven before the boat is engulfed and their lives lost will scarcely understand the principle that the value is in the struggle, not in the attainment. The homesickness of the religious man is in direct proportion to the earnestness and moral intensity of his life. Here is the Jerusalem of brass, of bluff and bluster, of empty pretentiousness, of want of conscience as the principle of success; there is the Jerusalem of gold. Here is misunderstanding and illusion triumphant; there is understanding and truth revealed. There love *is* love, sacrifice is known as sacrifice, unselfishness is not misunderstood as selfishness. The environment reflects the real, and every vestige of illusion is torn away; the life of the spirit is emancipated from its bonds.

The eternal does indeed impinge on the temporal, giving it whatever fullness of life it has, and making the present something more than an instant empty of content. But apart from the irreconcilable warfare between the loud tongues of the day and the still small voices of eternity, between the illusory valuations of the moment and the perspectives and point of view of the eternal, it remains the case that the eternal cannot adequately be embodied in time; the incommensurability remains even though its point of view triumphs. Hence it is in faith, and not in mystical immediacy of vision, that human beings living in time can grasp the eternal. Faith has indeed its confirmations; faith does succeed in organizing and unifying the life. But confirmation is not proof, and verification is never in time complete if the thing to be verified has any degree of concreteness or inclusiveness, as Professor Carnap [19] has lately said of the propositions of natural science. Taking human life and its highest aspirations as a whole, it therefore becomes true to say that eternity is the true verification.

Worldly wisdom assigns to struggle and hardship a finite teleology in time; religion as supernaturalism assigns to suffering and discipline an infinite teleology in eternity. Worldly wisdom says: Would Lincoln have become as great and distinguished and beloved of the people as he was, had he not been a rail splitter in his youth, and a struggling frontier lawyer in his early manhood? Would Garfield ever have become President of these United States had he not begun life as a canal boy? Only the most miserably worthless of all attitudes toward life has no abstraction, no power to sacrifice the near for the distant, living wholly in the moment, for the moment, and by the moment. But supernaturalism has an infinite abstraction, and assigns the whole of life to discipline and to struggle. It has the courage to risk totally, so that it stands to lose all or to gain all. Naturalism is the petty bourgeois calculation that fears to put all its eggs in one basket; its motto is, *Ne quid nimis,* too much and too little spoils everything. Supernaturalism knows only one evil and one good, but the difference is absolute; naturalism knows many evils and many goods, but the difference is merely relative. It is thus a flabbiness of spirit, a dissipation of energy; supernaturalism has the vigor of concentration, the energizing impetus of a single purpose. I do not know whether to laugh or to weep over the impudent commiseration with which the smallness of heart that dares not believe in the things God has prepared for them that love him speaks of the " compensatory " feebleness of otherworldliness; the assumed superiority with which an effeminacy that grasps impatiently for what lies nearest at hand dares to speak of the singleness of aim that puts the trivialities and the baubles aside to seek for the realities beyond is assuredly comic. It is in the spirit of a supernaturalistic religiosity that Kierkegaard everywhere emphasizes *decisiveness: either-or* is the key to heaven; *both-and* is the road to hell.

The novelists of a bygone age found the heroic in relation to their theme of love between the sexes in the period of courtship; in the struggle with uncertainty, with hard-hearted parents, or with unfavorable circumstances; in a still earlier age the naïve consciousness found a romantic-heroic interest in the conception of a fight with ogres and enchantments. The novelists of the present have ceased to believe in the heroic in relation to love; they find it interesting and intriguing only when seen against the background of marital unfaithfulness. Neither the innocent poesy of a bygone age nor the not-so-innocent poesy of the present, has any eye for the lifelong ethical struggle to which the truly religious individual commits himself in marriage, namely, to preserve for the whole of life, in just pride of feeling and decent loyalty of affection, the love that is the substantial core of every true marriage. It is this resolution for life that distinguishes a marriage from legalized mutual seduction; it is this assumption of responsibility for the preservation of affection that as the years pass sublimates it into something still nobler and higher, though it by no means ceases to be affection. While the passions of youth fade, and their illusions with them, the love that is determined as spirit grows only the stronger, for it alone partakes of the eternal.

Naturalism recognizes only finite satisfactions. It renounces the organization of life about a single aim, one having for its object the realization of a single infinite value intrinsic to the individual, the value that is the personality itself when standing in a concrete God relationship. All its values are finite and shifting; one replaces another, develops and is modified, and is again replaced in its turn; all are external to the individual himself, or intrinsic merely to some relativity of his being. His happiness is thus in the last analysis without and not within. Such a happiness is inevitably subject to the tragic reservation that attaches to all relative and differential goods, namely, the imperfections and inequalities of a differential distribution, one conditioned essentially by differences of talent, capacity, and circumstance. Naturalism knows of no happiness that is a happiness for all.

It is indeed true that the heroic in human life is inseparably bound up with struggle and striving rather than with present enjoyment, that the "divine discontent" is higher than the trivial and stupid contentment that is quite completely at home in the world. This is because the former is the only adequate expression for the actual situation of the individual in that *existence* which synthesizes the eternal and the temporal. Says Hamann: [20] "This anxious unrest in the world is the only proof of our heterogeneity. For if we wanted nothing we would make no more of our lives than do the heathen or the transcendental philosophers, who know nothing of God and stare themselves silly at the wonders of nature; no homesickness would lay hold on us. This importunate restlessness, this sacred hypochondria, is perhaps the fire with which we sacrificial victims must be salted and preserved against the corruption of the passing centuries."

An absent-minded naturalistic speculation, committing itself to a temporal immanence for all values, sometimes professes to believe that struggle is a higher category than victory, strain higher than rest. But because it lacks the concept of the eternal, it is in consequence committed to the paradox that striving everlastingly, without attainment, is a value per se. But to make seeking and struggling an end in itself is by no means in the spirit of a supernatural religion; it is indeed a nonsensical absurdity. It is our deepest demand upon life, ingrained in our human nature, that it promise and realize happiness; and realize, moreover, a justifiable happiness, one sharable by all, a happiness for man as man. Two such dissimilar thinkers as Plato and Nietzsche clasp hands across the centuries in affirmation of this truth. Plato says that war is for the sake of peace, and not for the sake of future wars; and he argues in the *Theaetetus* [21] that becoming is for the sake of being, and not vice versa. And is not Nietzsche's famous drunken song of Zarathustra built about the refrain that "all joys want eternity"? And so they do; or, rather, the deepest joy of human life is something that is of and by and for the eternal.

Faith in the eternal is what gives to the individual who has it the courage to be himself as over against the changing of fashions. He is relieved of the necessity of being "modern"; he is permitted to reflect that every error and aberration that we now condemn as belonging to the past was once "the very latest thing out." It gives him the steadfastness loyally and uncompromisingly to adhere to the principle of his life, and frees him from being timeserver and opportunist. It was the hope of better judges in another world, though the hope was merely a "perhaps," that helped Socrates to cling, with an uncompromisingness that was judged as arrogance, to the idea of his life when facing the judges of this world. When the stresses of life exceed the measure of a man's experience, it is the otherworldliness of faith that gives him victory over the world. The children of time, on the other hand, are indeed the children of time; they must needs follow the perishing and shifting fashions of this world. Under stress they are plunged into despair, as they were already in despair without knowing it; when the strains of life transcend their understanding of what is tolerable and reasonable to endure, their thought is of self-extinction.

Under the discipline of this-worldliness we have reached the point where we feel no shame in avowing that we cannot reasonably require of ourselves the realization of life's moral task until society and its economic system are so transformed that "the good man will no longer be penalized for his goodness." What a happy prospect for a prolonged moral holiday this gives us! For it will surely be a long time before we can expect a reorganization of society against the forces of entrenched selfishness on the one hand and the folly and self-delusions of the masses on the other, if men cannot be expected to strive for goodness until goodness can be had without striving, without self-discipline, and without cost — dirt-cheap at the price. To such depths of moral thoughtlessness have we descended in our day; or shall I regard this as one more indication of our uninterrupted progress?

If human life is to be kept from stagnation, it must be stirred by the vision of something higher. Man must have something that draws him "from above." He cannot lift himself by his bootstraps; there is no moral power in faith in ourselves. It is this something higher that supernaturalism finds and expresses; how strange to regard the reference of life to a divine source as mere dissipation of strength! And on the other hand how tragic the misunderstanding that transforms the interpretation of life in terms of the eternal into a mere dialectical exercise for logicians! Supernatural religion is the attempt to bring the point of view and the perspectives of the eternal to bear upon the affairs of time. This cannot be done on paper; it can be done only in the concrete present situation, on the street. He who thinks this to be an easy task, a flight from life, merely accuses himself of being one who has never tried it.

VII

The Transforming Power of Otherworldliness

This address was delivered originally on February 3, 1929, at a vesper service at Carleton College, Northfield, Minnesota, and has never before been published.

THE MODERN SPIRIT exerts two powerful pressures on the religious address. On the theoretical side it insists on placing in the foreground of attention the problem of assimilating modern knowledge. The religious address is tempted either to defend religion against a possible attack from this quarter or to seek support for religious ideas in the results of recent scientific research or in recent philosophical speculation. On the practical side there is a tendency to seek a justification for religion in the eyes of common sense, to enroll religion in the service of the wisdom of experience, and to show how valuable it is as an instrument of efficiency. The promise of godliness for the life to come retreats into the background; its promise for the life that now is monopolizes the attention; and — what is more significant still — the latter promise tends more and more to be so interpreted as to bring it into complete accord with that natural desire for success which is so deep-rooted in human beings.

These influences exert their pressure upon the present speaker as upon others. Nor have I any wish to condemn them unqualifiedly as temptations to be shunned or evils to be resisted. The search for intellectual clarity has its obvious and genuine significance, and much that may be said about the contributions of religion to efficiency and energy in the business of life seems to me just and sound. But the tendency to an exclusive preoccupation with such considerations is another matter. This cannot but tend to obscure the distinctiveness of the religious message, and the qualitative heterogeneity of the religious principles.

Religion claims a place in human life, but the place it claims is not one of tolerance, but of supremacy. True religion does not borrow significance from other forms of human culture; it does not ask to be supported either by science or by art, although it makes free to utilize both for its own distinctive ends. It does not wish to be impressed into the service of a kind of well-being or happiness external to its own spirit; it seeks to vivify and transform these conceptions themselves, and thus to be the arbiter of human valuations. It is, in brief, the master passion. It seeks control of "all thoughts, all passions, all delights, whatever stirs this mortal frame"; it strives to make all human activities its ministers — servants that feed the sacred flame of faith.

To speak otherwise of religion is to rob it of its spirit of aggressiveness. But the aggressiveness of religion is so much its very heart and soul that it cannot be defended or patronized without suffering betrayal. And yet it happens, strangely enough, that its representatives sometimes appear in the role of insinuating beggars, seeking the crumbs that fall from the table of the scientist or the philosopher or the worldly-wise man. In its truth, however, the religious spirit is a bestowing spirit, capable of making all rich, both rich and poor.

In this conviction I have chosen to speak this evening on the power exerted in human life by the spirit of otherworldliness. I do not mean to deny the significance of this-worldliness, or that religion has a this-worldly aspect. On the contrary, I claim for religion an inclusiveness, a suppleness, a quality of penetration, an absolute commensurability, which makes it at home in every situation. But it is my conviction that these two aspects of life, this-worldliness on the one side and otherworldliness on the other, are in their truth to be valued as the relative is to the absolute, the subordinate to the dominant, the many things useful to the one thing needful. Take away from life every relation to the absolute, and the relative itself is puffed up into the semblance of an importance that it cannot sustain. Take away from life every relation to the absolute, and the relativities of life lose their adequate ordering principle; life tends to become an anarchic chaos, or " a tale . . . full of sound and fury, signifying nothing."

Before proceeding with this talk, I wish to acknowledge my indebtedness to one of the great religious thinkers of all time, the Danish philosopher Søren Kierkegaard, whose name, although he has been dead three quarters of a century, is still practically unknown to English-speaking people, nor have any of his numerous works as yet found their way into English. Because he created a new religious philosophy which stressed the category of the individual and his relation to God, and showed that truth can exist only in subjectivity, I feel that he is destined to exert a powerful ethical and religious influence upon future thinking, and I am therefore glad to afford you a brief introduction to some phases of his thought by drawing freely upon the ideas he set forth in one of his edifying discourses, entitled, " The Expectation of an Eternal Happiness," published in 1844; and by paraphrasing certain passages I shall try to give you some idea of the clarity, the simplicity, and the earnestness with which

Kierkegaard appealed "to that individual" whom he was happy to call "my reader." Hence, employing the same text as did Kierkegaard, I call your attention to certain moving words of the Apostle Paul, which you will find in his Second Letter to the Corinthians, words that express the conviction embodied in my theme:

"Wherefore we faint not; but though our outward man is decaying, yet our inward man is renewed day by day. For our light affliction, which is for the moment, worketh for us more and more exceedingly an eternal weight of glory; while we look not at the things which are seen, but at the things which are not seen: for the things which are seen are temporal; but the things which are not seen are eternal."

These words of Paul testify to a conviction which his life gloriously interprets. The principle of this conviction is the thoroughgoing interpenetration of life with the consciousness of the eternal, the bringing of the invisible everywhere to bear upon the visible, finding in the eternal the ultimate ground and the final clarification of human life.

The modern spirit is not indisposed to admire the boldness of Paul's faith, but it hesitates to follow in his footsteps. Its reasons are multifarious, but chief among them is the lurking fear that such faith is, after all, a retreat from life into the realm of fancy. It must be admitted that we are all of us confronted with this danger, a danger that presents itself not in one form only but in many, not only when life is professedly religious, but also when life is thoroughly secularized. Imaginary compensations for actual weakness, the selfish and cowardly indulgence in daydreams that but increase that weakness more and more, sapping the soul's vitality — these are a sickness of the soul which may threaten to become a sickness unto death. The spirit of otherworldliness in religion is not only intolerant of this weakness but is an actual cure for it. The hope of eternal bliss is for Paul not a refuge from life; it is a challenge to live yet more deeply and intensely. The essence of daydreaming is the separation of the imagination from the will, its development in isolation from the rest of life. The essence of a religious faith in an external order is its transforming power over the rest of life, an influence that dares ignore no single detail as too small or unimportant. The eternal presses instantly upon the will; its motto is: " Work . . . while it is day "; " Now is the acceptable time." If the expectation of the eternal does not work this result upon the life, it is a counterfeit expectation and not a genuine faith, a credulous superstition, an unclarified yearning, an affectation, an insincerity, a sick soul's flight from life, not a sound soul's sincere presence in the temporal.

Those who do not share the enthusiasm of this faith naturally regard it as an illusion. Nevertheless, it must not be forgotten that faith in the eternal arises like the phoenix out of the ashes of all the soul's previous illusions. It supersedes not only the happy illusions of childhood and the beautiful illusions of youth, the illusion of a romantic love that is happiness without responsibility; the illusions of maturity, which center about fame and money, power and success; but also the most persistent and deep-seated of all illusions, the illusion of self-adequacy and self-righteousness. This supersession is that dying away from the world of which religion speaks, a dying that conditions the life that is life indeed; the pain of this dying is mingled with the joy of this living; and this most significant of all the struggles that life affords is the supreme test of the reality of the soul's thoughts and aims and feelings.

Human life sometimes affords us a glimpse of an aesthetic perfection from which this deeper struggle seems to be excluded. The life of creative art, for example, appears to have a perfection of unity that knows nothing of the deep cleft between preparation and consummation. Each step or phase of such an activity seems both an end in itself, yielding its own immanent satisfaction, as well as a transition to the equally significant next step or stage. But such experiences are fortunate episodes in life, not expressive of its essential structure. They are imperfect analogues, foreshadowing dimly that deeper harmony which can enter into the present life only by anticipation and faith. Man is a duality;[22] such is the testimony of one of the greatest thinkers of antiquity, whose mythical genealogy of Eros as the child of Poverty and Plenty, who because of his participation in this double nature is always striving, desiring, seeking for that which in its fullness is beyond the present self, is an imaginative fancy meant as an essential picture of human life.

Such is also the testimony of Paul, who makes human life a synthesis of the temporal and the eternal, faith the anticipation that knits them together, eternity the true fulfillment. Time separates the way from the goal to which it leads; it separates means from ends, preparation from consummation. Every more earnest view of life acknowledges the significance of this separation; only frivolity expects to reap its harvest the instant it has sown. The more ambitious the view of life, the more remote the consummation that it proposes; this principle is, in general, the measure both of the worth of the striving and of the significance of the reward sought. The religious view of life is the most ambitious of all; it is charged with a demand upon life that makes even the most beautiful temporal consummation seem a sorry imperfection, if it is to be *the* consummation. It disposes of an enthusiasm that is content to make, not a longer or shorter period within time, but the entire earthly life a state of striving and of preparation. The religious man confesses to the view that life is a way, that a man is, in his true character, a pilgrim; he looks toward an unseen city, "a house not made with hands, eternal, in the heavens." In testimony of this he calls himself a believer, which means in his mouth what the staff signifies in the wayfarer's hands, namely, "What I seek is not yet here."

Let us now consider this view of life from a variety of aspects in order that we may be enabled to grasp more clearly the part that it plays in human life; the difference that is made, the power that is exerted, by the expectation of an eternal life and an eternal joy.

First, let us note that this expectancy gives to our lives their greatest possible tension, since it evokes the maximum interest. To bestow an infinite interest upon a finite value is the torturing self-contradiction of the mere worldly life. It is not only hope that is found to be precarious, but experience teaches us that the things hoped for deceive us even though they be attained. The fulfillment at hand, we ask ourselves, "Is *this* the consummation I so devoutly wished?" The eternal alone can furnish the true objective for that infinite interest which God has implanted as a potentiality in the heart of man. And, conversely, it is the evocation of this interest which constitutes the core of the true belief in immortality. Where this passion is atrophied or suppressed, the idea of immortality is a mere luxury, an unmeaning decorative addition to the surface of life, an affectation and a fancy. It is this deep and vital interest that is the oil in the lamps of all those who wait the coming of the bridegroom, the neglect of which excludes one from participation in the marriage feast; for an infinite personal interest is the subjective form for an indwelling of the eternal. When once the possibility of such an interest has dawned upon man's horizon, he is confronted with a challenge which he cannot evade or deny without doing violence to his deeper self; this glimpse of immortality makes a belief in it morally necessary, in the same sense that a philosopher once said of God that if God is possible,[23] then he is also necessary.

Let us also note that the consciousness of immortality removes the last vestige of abstractness, of casualness, of the possibility of subterfuge and evasion from man's relationship to God, and reveals life in its absolute earnestness. A transitory relation has in it the seeds of unreality. God's immanence in the world and in the human consciousness is an invisible presence; it does not have the immediately obvious or compelling character of an external or sensible reality. His omnipresence is therefore a seeking, a questioning, a solicitation — a courting, if you will, of man's free spirit; and this unobtrusive courtship is the most tremendous concession conceivable to man's independence. But lest this concession become a mere weakness on the part of God, a sheer madness, it must be permeated by the condition of an inescapable responsibility on the part of man. But if, after a lifetime of evasion and neglect, I can end all by simply tucking myself away in a grave, and be as if neither I nor God had ever been, then God has permitted himself to be mocked, and life is not real and earnest to the last degree. But God is not mocked, and it is for this reason also that he is not the God of the dead, but of the living. The true faith in immortality is thus nurtured in fear and trembling.

The expectation of immortality presents to the individual an ideal goal in which he can be concretely present, because it is a goal in whose attainment he himself participates.

There are views of life that seek to enhance its ideal significance by setting the individual a task whose realization is placed beyond the individual life, in some future period of mankind or of the world. This view makes all the preceding generations of men mere instruments, not ends in themselves; it arbitrarily selects a particular generation, or a group of generations, to be the fortunate beneficiaries of an effort which they have not shared, and permits them to reap where they have not sown. The concept of the progress of the race doubtless has its relative meaning and justification; but alone and by itself as the highest good, it is a mere abstraction. If, on the other hand, every human being has his ideal goal in himself, and if this self is no mere particularistic entity but a true individual, at one and the same time itself and the human race, so that men cannot without humanity be made perfect, then there is established an immanent end for man, which makes him no mere instrument, and makes of his life something higher than slavery in the service of external ends. And the human race too becomes something more than an intellectual abstraction, as it is in the historical process; in the relationship of each and every man to the eternal, the human race as such becomes a concrete reality.

The expectation of immortality has the power to reconcile every human being to his neighbor, his friend, and his foe, in a common understanding of the essential in life. It unites him to his fellow men in the most profound of all sympathies, and in the only thinkable universal goal. Every other goal is to a greater or less extent divisive, depends upon differences, and establishes invidious distinctions, not forgetting the invidious distinction between those who are privileged to give and those who are foredoomed merely to receive. But the expectation of immortality is not relevant to differential talent or fortunate circumstances; it establishes itself upon the basis of our common humanity, and no one is excluded who does not exclude himself. It cultivates no stoic insensibility; it acknowledges the genuineness of relative goods, but it denies that they constitute the perfection of life. It looks, therefore, toward a more perfect life, in which all men will have all things; in which God, who is all in all, will by the miracle of his love be present whole and entire in every single human heart. To believe something like this, so it seems to me, is to be human. And believing this, one may learn to wear his differences lightly, as if they were but the disguising cloak for the royal purple of humanity beneath.

The expectation of an eternal issue for human life will also help to liberate a man from the ruinous illusion that the quality of the means he chooses is of less importance than the ends he seeks. It is of the essence of the eternal, as the goal of life, that method and end are always in exact and perfect harmony. The methods, on the contrary, by which any temporal end may be attained, are diverse and incommensurable, and the choice of means becomes more or less a matter of indifference. He who stakes everything upon his success in attaining such ends will in the last analysis succumb to necessity that knows no law. Every ethical principle will tend to become for him vacillating and uncertain. Honesty is the best policy — aye, in most circumstances perhaps — at any rate the appearance of honesty, if not the reality, and a certain degree of honesty, if not its utmost perfection. And so with every other ethical principle; it must not be applied too severely, lest it defeat its own ends and fail to be justified by the results. The maxim of a worldly prudence is therefore always *ne quid nimis,* to carry nothing to extremes. It has no sympathy

with that divine madness, the transcendent enthusiasm,
which breaks through the confines of a petty calculation,
because it derives its strength from the eternal and the unchanging. The statesman permits himself an appeal to the
lower levels of character and intelligence, and thus abdicates
his leadership before he enters upon it, because he fears that
any other course would jeopardize an immediate success.
All who make it their highest aim to secure for themselves
any form of external power — kings and emperors and
statesmen and demagogues and ecclesiastics and sophists —
have not scrupled to exploit and foster human weakness and
illusions, its prejudices, and its basest passions. They boast
of taking the world as they find it; it cannot escape a
thoughtful contemplation that they also leave the world in
essentially the same situation. Not so the saints, the apostles,
the prophets, and the martyrs, the men and women who
have yielded allegiance to an eternal order, and have dedi-
cated their lives to bear witness for the truth. Concession
and distortion might have brought them a tremendous success; but they lived for eternity, and hence chose rather the
threat of failure and the certainty of opposition. And eternity knows them, and acknowledges them for its own. In
the perspective of the moment, success is everything, and
failure is failure; in the longer perspective of history, the
immediate success is already of lesser importance, and the
failure of the moment is sometimes the success of the future;
in the perspective of eternity, success is nothing and failure
is nothing, but the spirit of endurance in suffering and
loyalty in striving for a good cause is everything. The expectation of the eternal will help a man to be steadfast and
true to his cause; it will help him to understand the difference between the devotion that serves a cause and the calculation that attaches itself to a cause in order to be served

by it; and it will habituate in him the search for the most glorious harmony of human life, the harmony of the means with their corresponding end.

The expectation of the eternal will help a man to be contemporary with himself in time, and wean him from the paralyzing effort of trying to shoulder the vaguely looming burden of tomorrow, or of all the tomorrows, in place of a concentration of effort and attention upon the definitely restricted burden of today. The power to concern himself with the future is a mark of man's kinship with the divine. For if there were no future, there would be no past, and if there were no past and no future, man would be hidebound in his instincts and a child of the moment, his horizon no broader and his head no higher than that of the beast that perishes. The struggle with the future is therefore an ennobling struggle, and no man can conquer the present who has not first conquered the future. But how can a man conquer the future before he has fought with the present? Only through that expectation of victory which is of the essence of faith in the eternal. This expectation is no mere youthful buoyancy, no mere confident self-appraisal. It is an expectation of a victory that transcends both success and defeat, both happiness and sorrow. It is the assurance that all things work together for good to them that love God. When the future has been conquered in this sense and in this sign, then and only then can the individual soberly and without illusion be wholly present in the present task, in each successive moment contemporary with himself.

Finally, let us note that the expectation of an eternal happiness gives a man a measuring rod, a standard of estimation, which will help him to understand himself in time, as over against the extremes of stress and strain, of fortune and misfortune. The wisdom of experience yields some such standard, and is useful in estimating the individual moments of life, mediating an adjustment to them that lends to man some degree of poise and equanimity. But this wisdom is based upon the individual and the particular, upon the partial and the discrete; the measure that it yields is a restricted and finite measure, the application of its standard confined within a limited compass and sphere. Whenever a man's soul is pregnant with the expectation of the eternal, this measure becomes for him too small and petty; he may thus, unwisely, be tempted to reject its relative aid. But neither can he fall back upon the romantic standards of youth. Whoever has only a finite standard of evaluations has a life that is wholly a child of time, and cannot even be assured of his ability to cope with the finite, since it is always possible that events will break that his experience cannot help him to surmount. If this happens, he becomes the prey of despair. Whoever has experienced this has learned from experience that experience is not enough. But he who cherishes in his soul the lively expectation of an eternal joy has in that expectation a measure that is always adequate and always valid. By means of this standard he will be enabled to understand himself in times of stress and strain, when life's demands exceed the measure of a finite understanding, and the wisdom of experience breaks under a pressure it cannot bear. He will not permit success or happiness to rob him of this eternally valid standard, and substitute in its place the false and transient standards of vanity and conceit; he will not permit sorrow and suffering to impose upon him their false standards, and teach him the despairing grief that knows no hope.

" For our light affliction, which is for the moment, worketh for us more and more exceedingly an eternal weight of glory." Let us imagine for a moment that we know nothing more about the author of these words than the fact that he had said them. And let us assume that we tried, as well as we knew how, to infer from these words what sort of life must have fallen to his lot — to the lot of one who could give this earthly life and the life to come such a testimony. Doubtless we should conclude, should we not, that this man's life must have been relatively quiet and uneventful, a life in honorable obscurity, far from the turmoil and stress of great crises, not perhaps entirely unaware of that secret wisdom which suffering bestows upon its initiates, but nevertheless not tried in the extremes of physical danger and mental anguish. We should perhaps be reminded of another saying of apparently similar purport and background, namely, "that the earth is beautiful enough as a country to travel through, but not so beautiful as to make the wayfarer forget that he is on his way." And, having drawn this or a similar conclusion, let us suppose that someone then outlines for us, as if for the first time, the story of Paul's life. He tells us of Paul's spiritual trial on the road to Damascus, when he was made to reverse his whole concept of right and wrong, and hence evidently was a man not without experience of the soul's supreme crisis; he tells us of Paul's mystical exaltation and rapture, his being lifted up into the third heaven — and so we see that Paul was doubtless tempted to conceive a distaste for the ordinary humdrum course of life; he tells us that Paul was often heard to testify with an enthusiasm that made him seem a madman; that for the many years of an active life he was without home and without security, a scandal in the eyes of his compatriots, a fool to the Greeks, an outcast from the world, often in danger to life, experienced in hunger and nakedness, often in prison, and at last executed as a criminal.

Would not this narration tend to shake us out of ourselves, our poise and our equanimity, and extort from our lips the exclamation that such a life was not to be endured — an everlasting strain and the heaviest affliction? The standards of our experience would break down under the attempt to compass and to estimate such a life. But Paul had an eternal goal, and an eternally valid measure; hence it is that where we speak of a heavy and unendurable burden, he spoke of "a light affliction, which is for the moment." When the storms of life threatened to overwhelm him, Paul looked toward his goal, and measured the storms with his standard, and behold, they became light and momentary afflictions! When experience failed to help him, when its wisdom fell short of the demands of life, then his faith leaped to the rescue, laying hold of a joy and peace beyond all understanding.

When the stress of life transcends the measure of experience, and plunges worldly wisdom into the depths of despair, human life becomes a chaotic turmoil, without comfort and without hope, unless the hope of an eternal weight of glory brings into our lives its order and its calm. This is that genuine transvaluation of all values which religion through its otherworldliness brings to life: not the fantastic transvaluation of an imaginary superman, but the simple faith of common men and women, a faith, however, from which no genius need be excluded unless he excludes himself.

Notes

Inasmuch as the chapters here included were delivered as addresses, and hence usually were not annotated, some notes have been added for the convenience of the reader. In the case of allusions to Kierkegaard some references have been given to passages which, while not being direct quotations, suggest a similar thought. Where the author's name is not cited, the reference is to Kierkegaard's works.

CHAPTER I. THE DIGNITY OF HUMAN LIFE

[1] Suggested by Emerson's "So nigh is grandeur to our dust." *Voluntaries.*

[2] *Postscript*, 124.

[3] *Gospel of Suffering*, 174–177.

[4] *Postscript*, 327, 328.

[5] *Postscript*, 226.

CHAPTER II. PROGRESS IN RELIGIOUS THOUGHT

[6] Recalling Lessing's jesting reply to Jacobi. *Postscript*, 94.

[7] *Postscript*, 386–408; *Gospel of Suffering*, 103–117.

[8] *Fragments*, Ch. IV.

CHAPTER IV. FUNCTIONS OF INTELLIGENCE

[9] Edith Cavell, executed by the Germans in World War I, for espionage.

[10] Tennyson, in "Locksley Hall."

[11] A misquotation, in that Emerson uses "beauty" instead of "soul."

CHAPTER V. OBJECTIVE UNCERTAINTY AND HUMAN FAITH

[12] *Postscript*, 267–307.

[13] *Postscript*, 189, 190.

[14] *Philosophical Fragments*, 60–62; *Something About Kierkegaard*, by David F. Swenson, 234, 235.

[15] *Postscript*, 122, 385; *Edifying Discourses*, Vol. IV, Ch. I.

CHAPTER VI. SUPERNATURALISM — SOURCE OF MORAL POWER

[16] *Postscript*, 119, 352, 353.

[17] *Postscript*, 201–203.

[18] *Postscript*, 506, 507.

[19] In a paper entitled "Testability and Meaning," *Philosophy of Science*, Vol. III, No. 4, and Vol. IV, No. 1.

[20] Quoted by Kierkegaard in *Concept of Dread*, 145.

[21] *Theaetetus*, 153.

CHAPTER VII. THE TRANSFORMING POWER OF OTHERWORLDLINESS

[22] Plato, *Symposium; Postscript*, 54.

[23] Voltaire.